BLACK
AND BEAUTIFUL

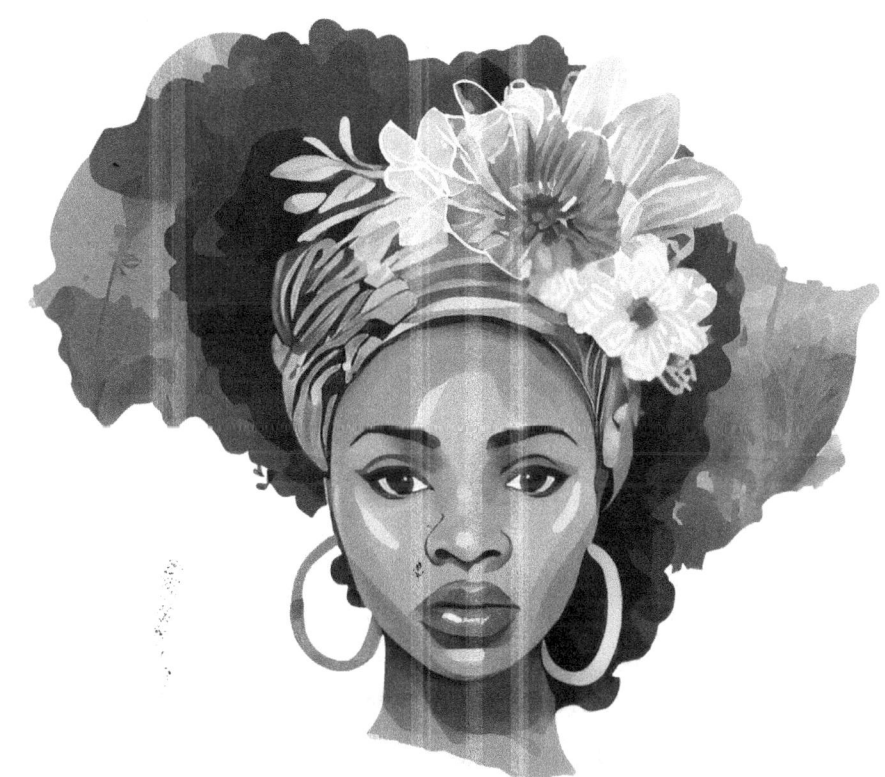

COLORING BOOK
WITH POSITIVE MOTIVATIONS

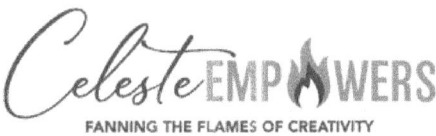

Celeste EMP WERS

FANNING THE FLAMES OF CREATIVITY

ISBN: 9798377368694

Printed in the United States of America

225-286-2856
www.celesteempowers.com
chortazoarts.com

About this coloring book

This coloring book was designed to allow you to relax, refresh, and be empowered through these beautiful pages. According to The Cleveland Clinic, "coloring can relax the brain." Other experts share the therapeutic benefits of art in reducing the activity of fear in the brain. It also reduces stress and allows you to think more clearly.

My prayer is that the combination of coloring and positive statements will help reduce your fears, lift your spirit and encourage you to be the best you possible.

Happy coloring,

Celeste Payne

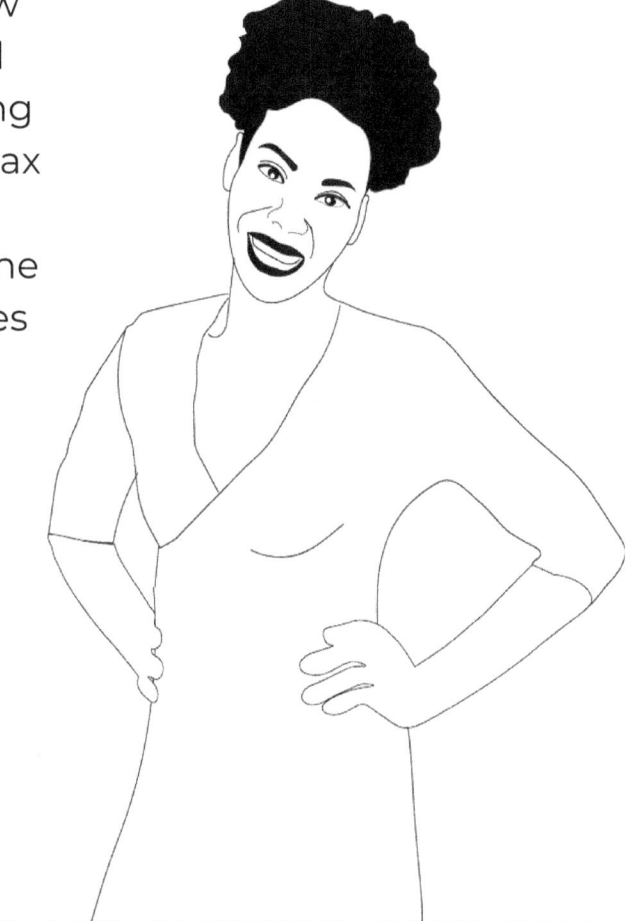

About the Author

Celeste Payne is an artist, educator, author, speaker, therapeutic art life coach, and art gallery owner. She offers in-person and virtual art classes and workshops and paint parties for youth and adults.

Her passion, however, is to help those who have experienced setbacks to Advance, Resurge, and Thrive using the arts as a highway to life transformation. By using her classes, books, group coaching, and global network of leaders, she inspires and supports women on their journey to personal, professional, and entrepreneurial success by helping them tap into their innate creativity.

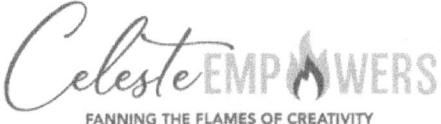
FANNING THE FLAMES OF CREATIVITY

www.celesteempowers.com

https://health.clevelandclinic.org/3-reasons-adult-coloring-can-actually-relax-brain/
https://www.beaumont.org/health-wellness/blogs/health-benefits-of-coloring-for-adults

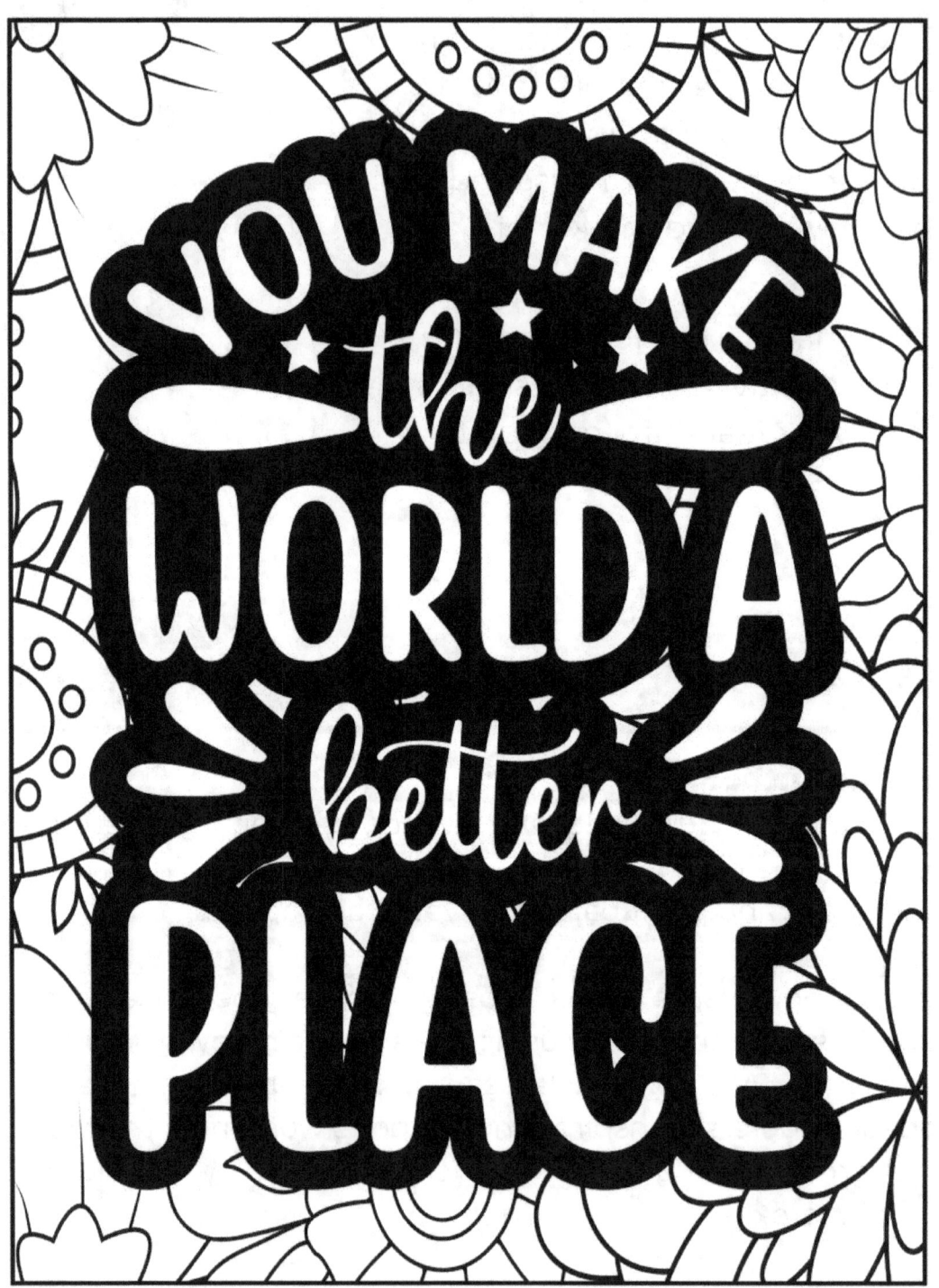

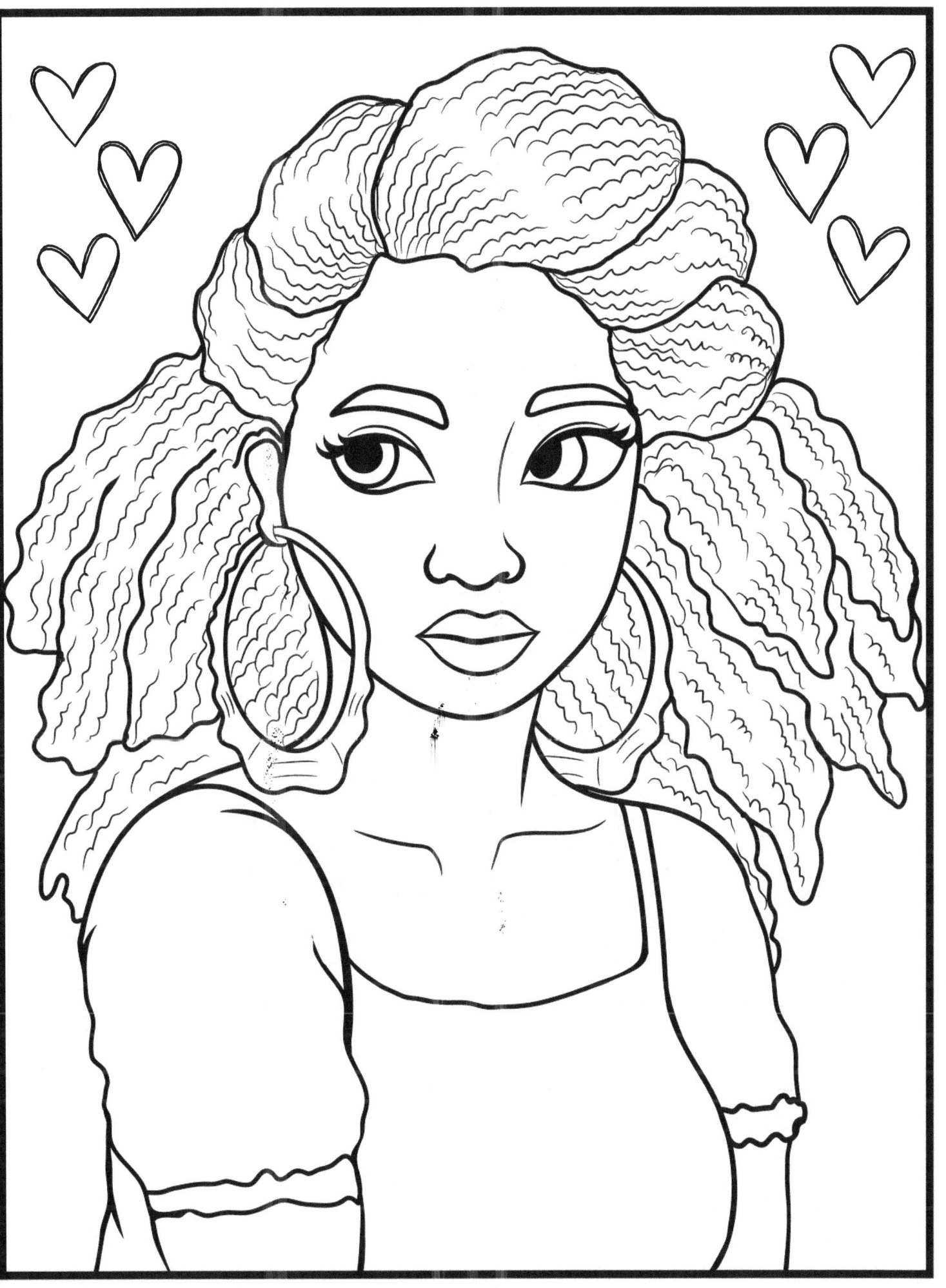

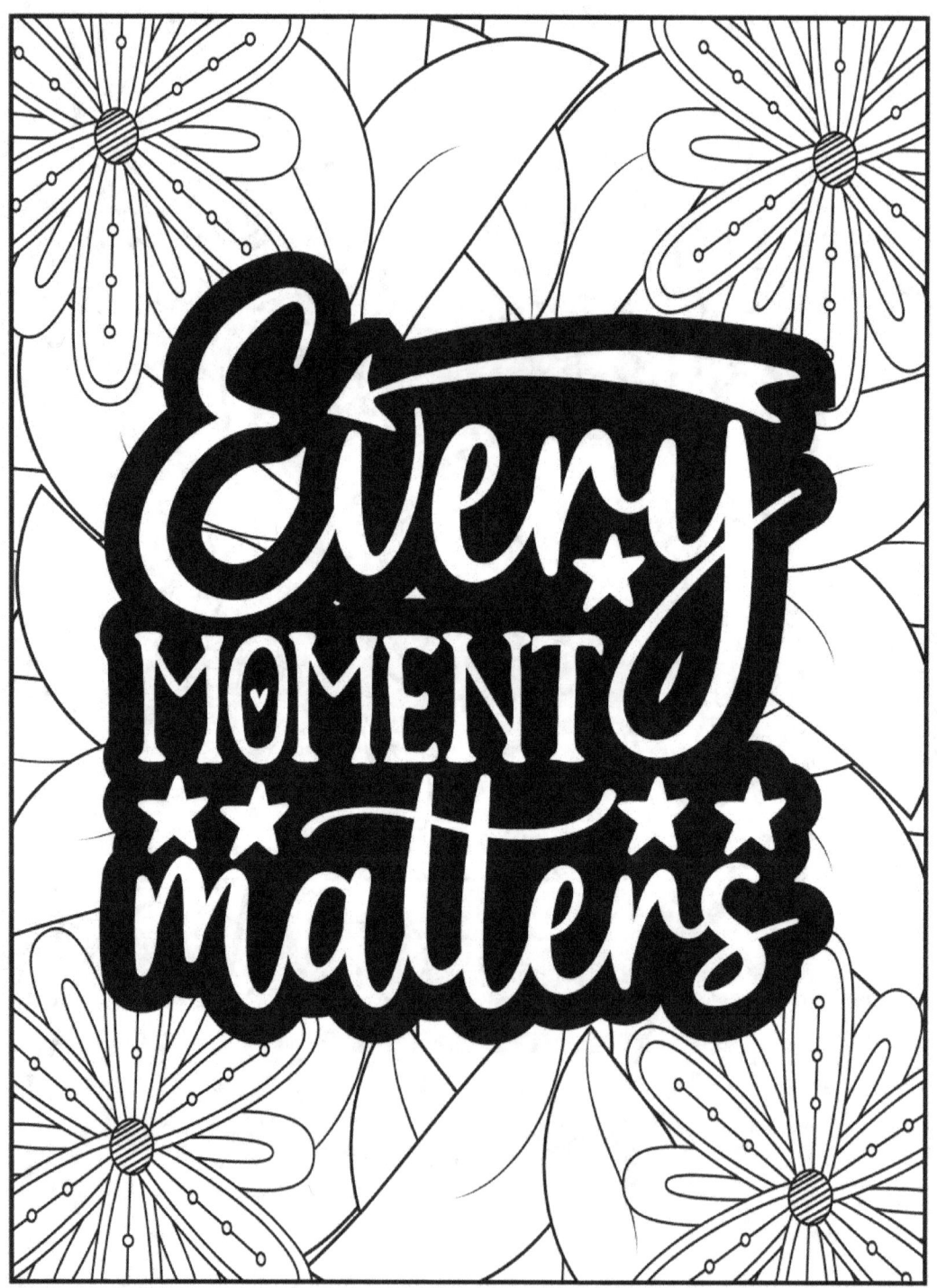

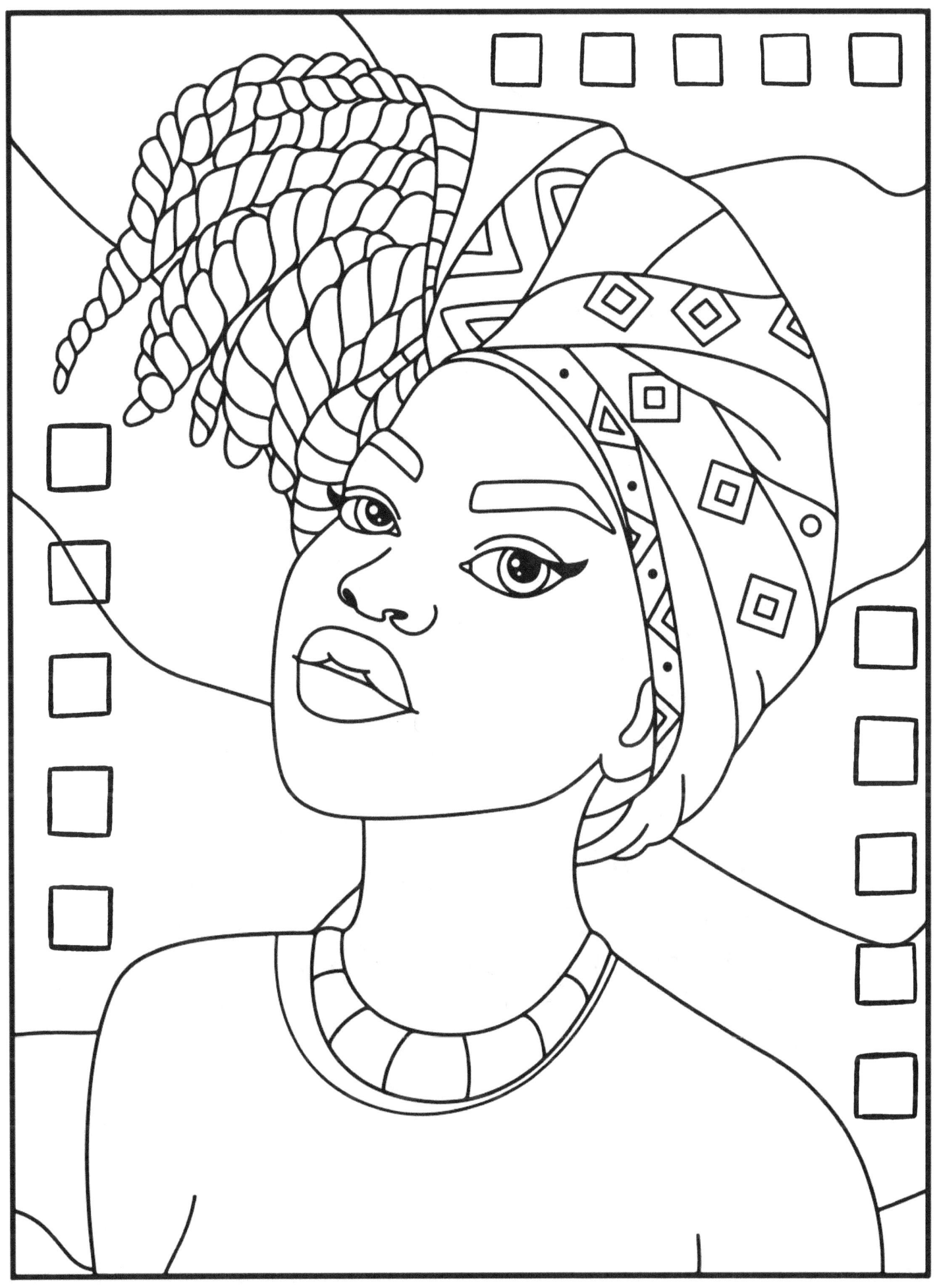

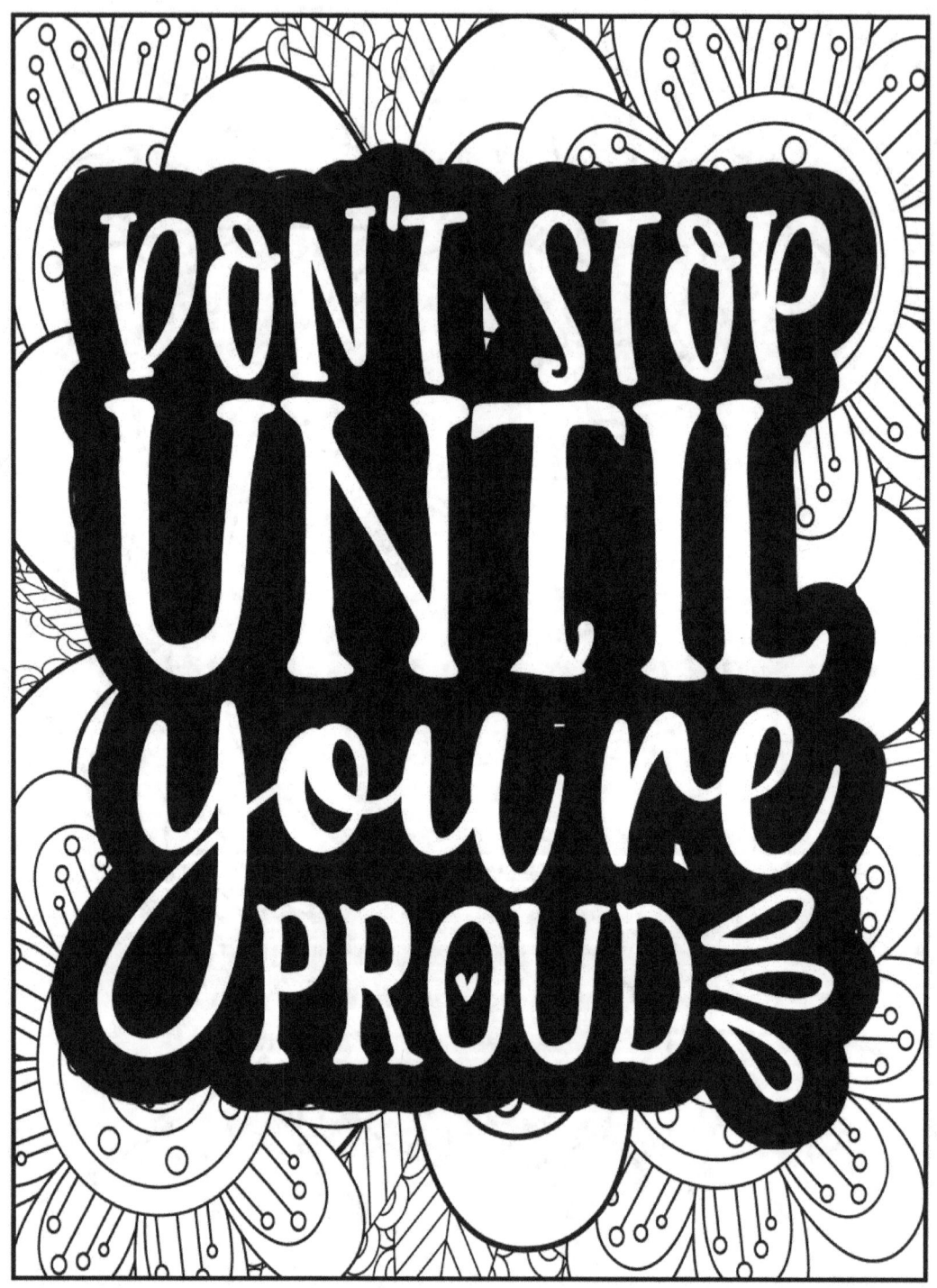

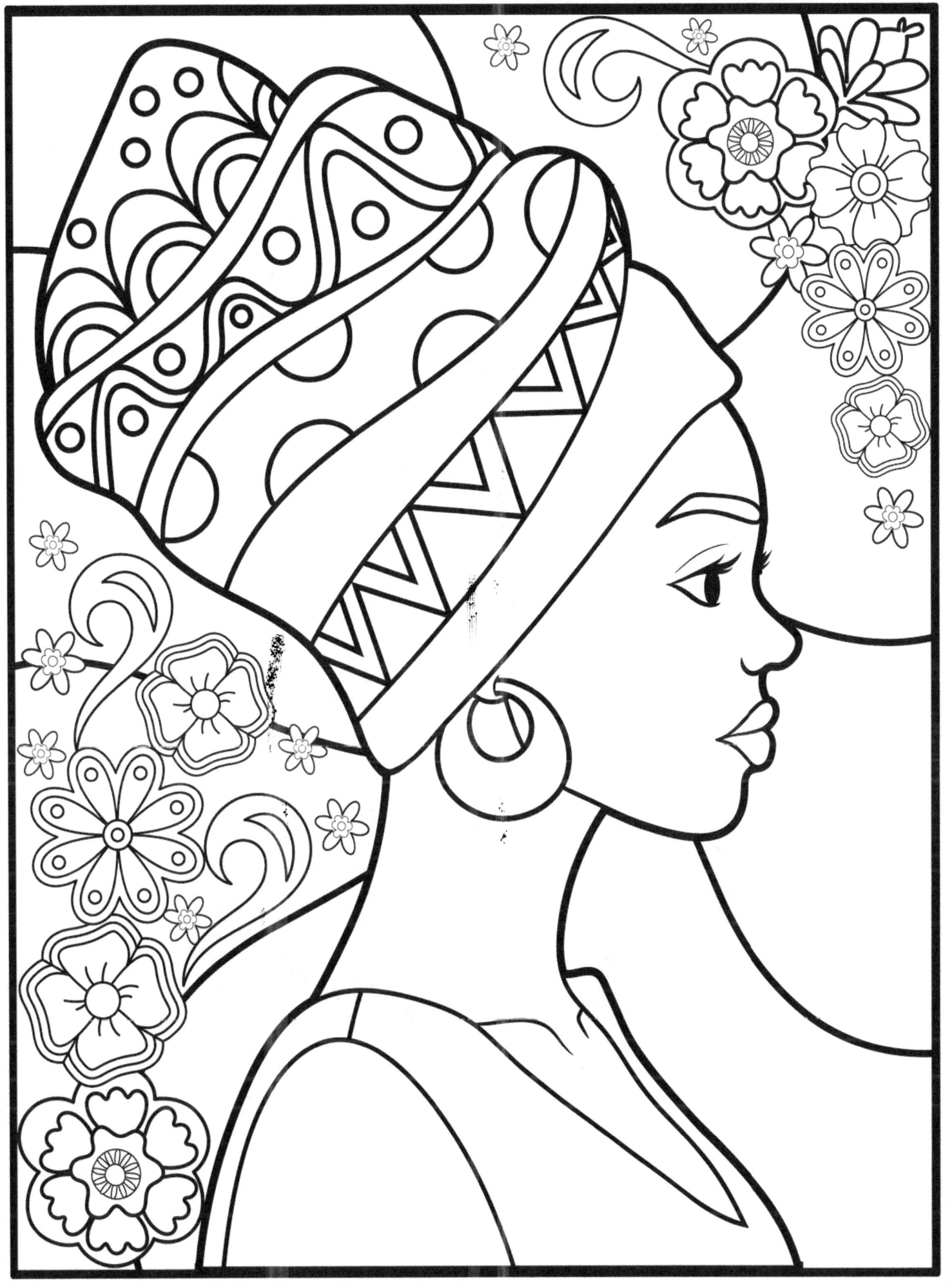

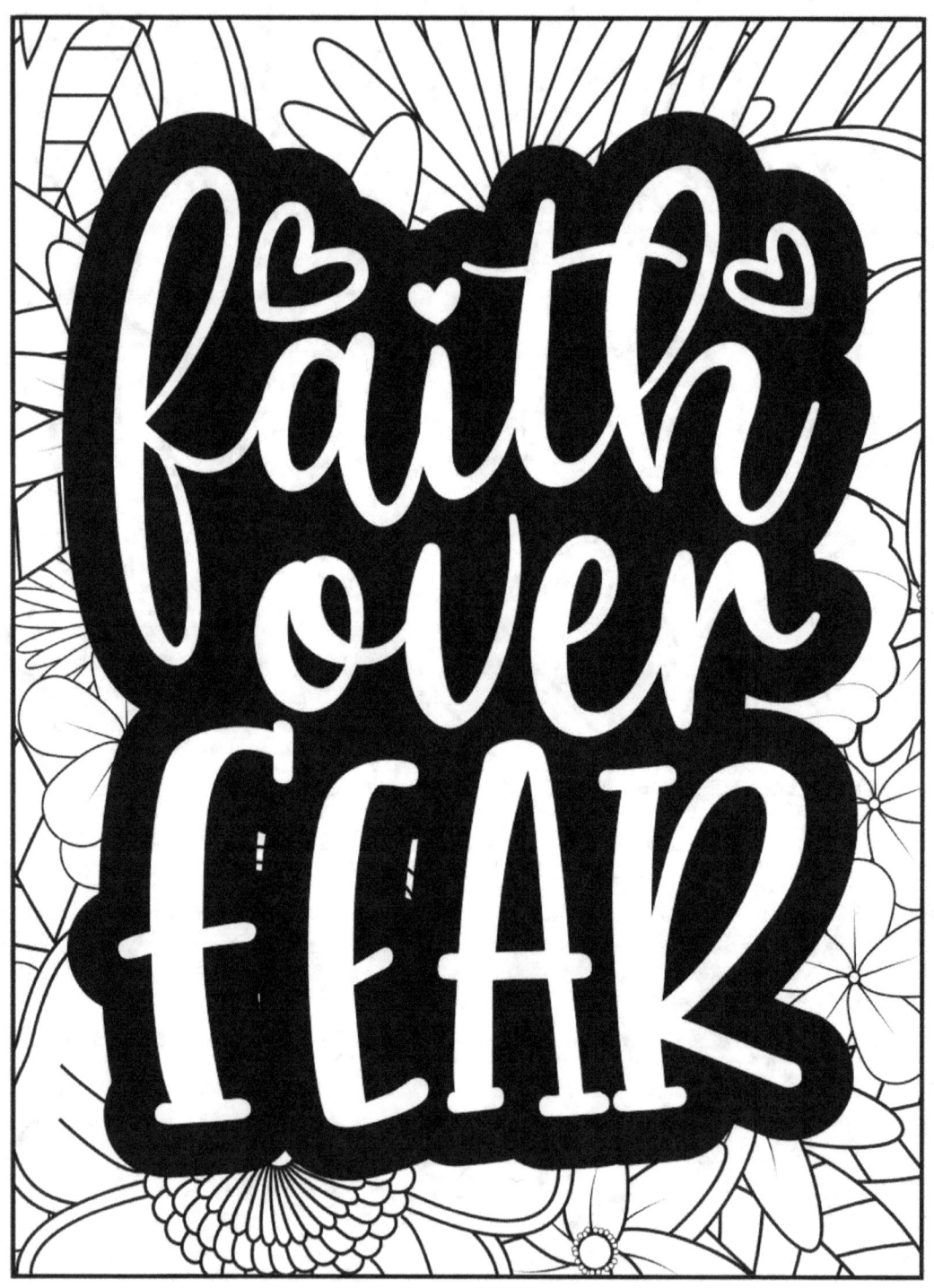

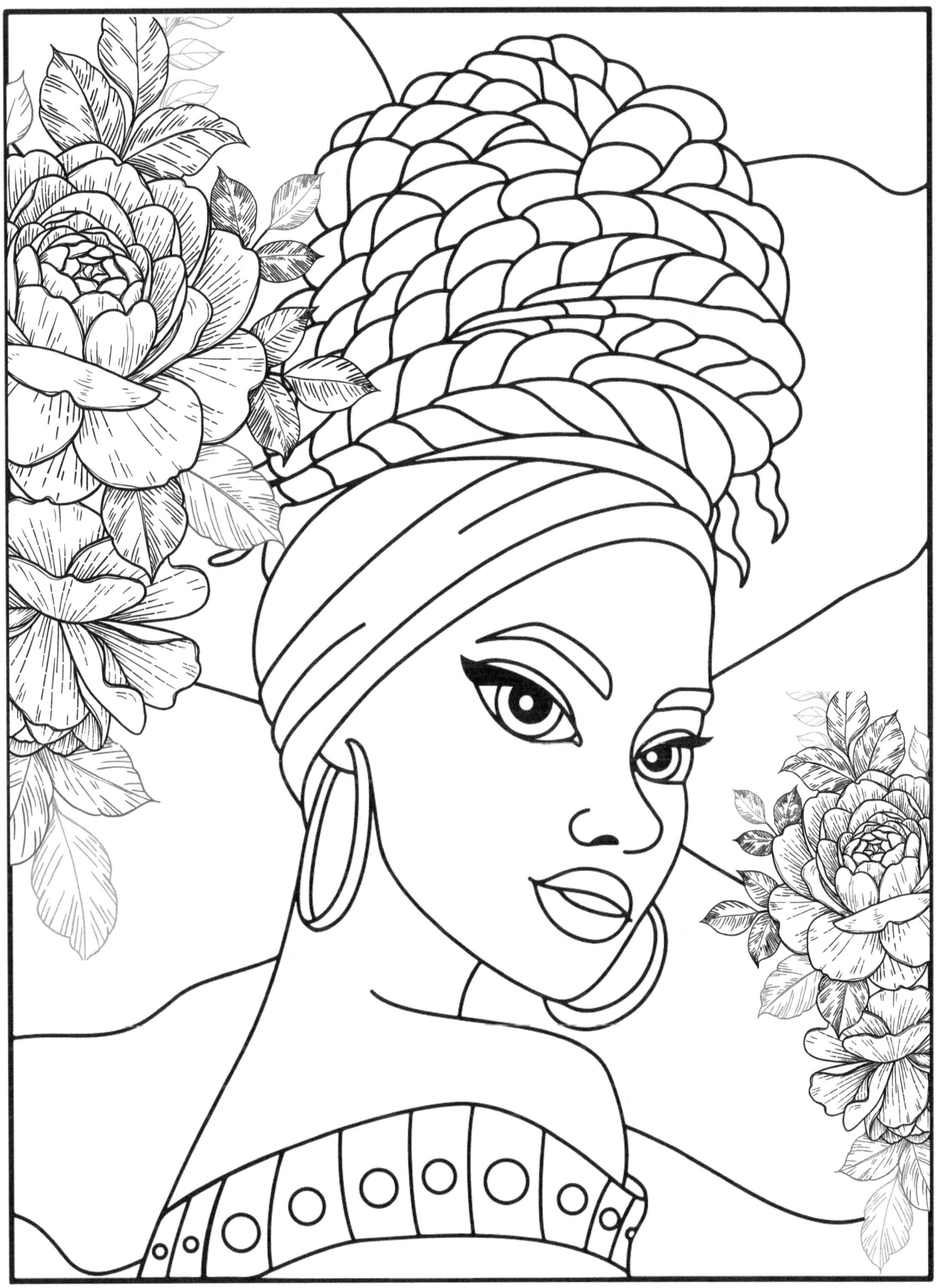

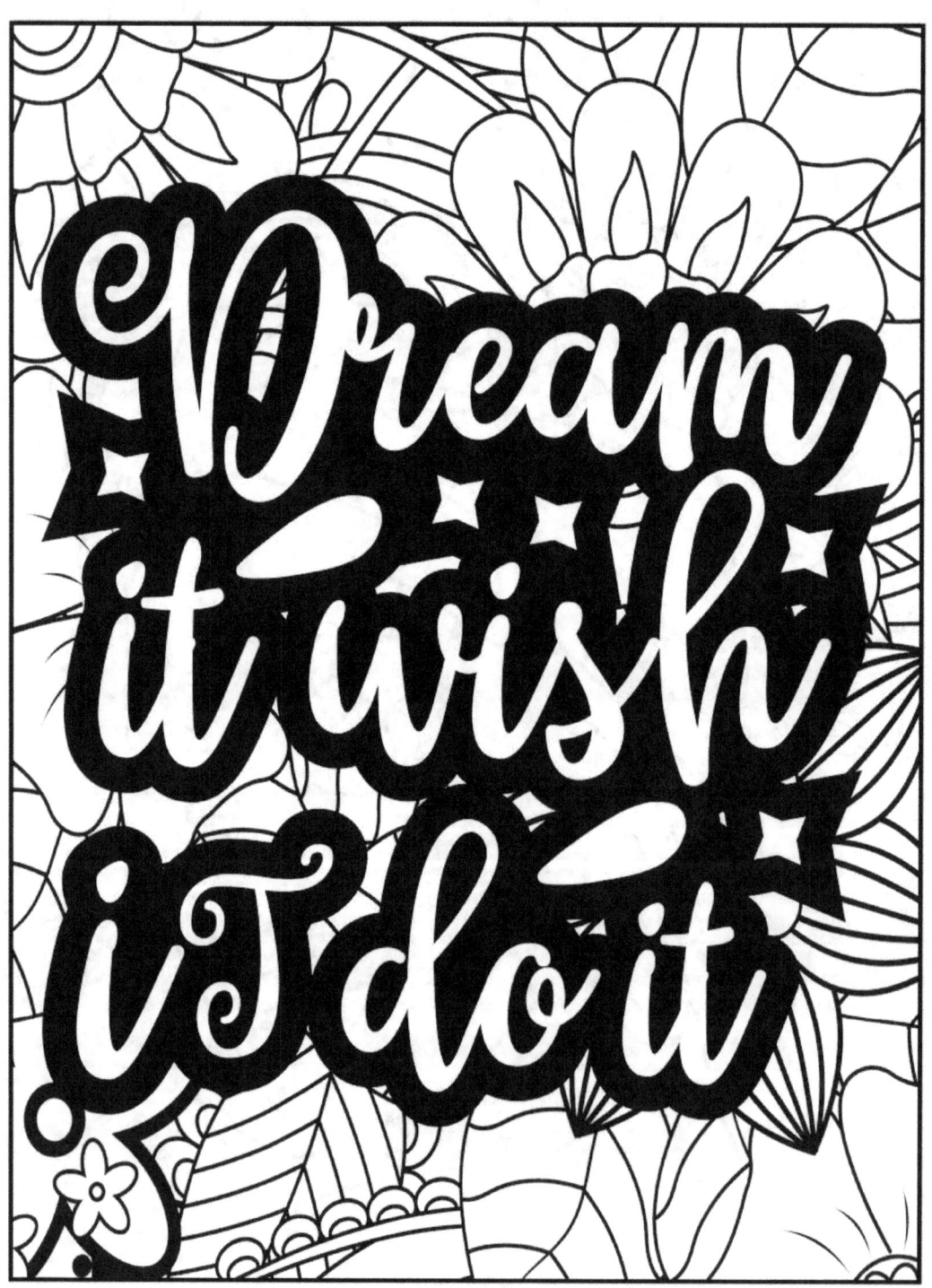

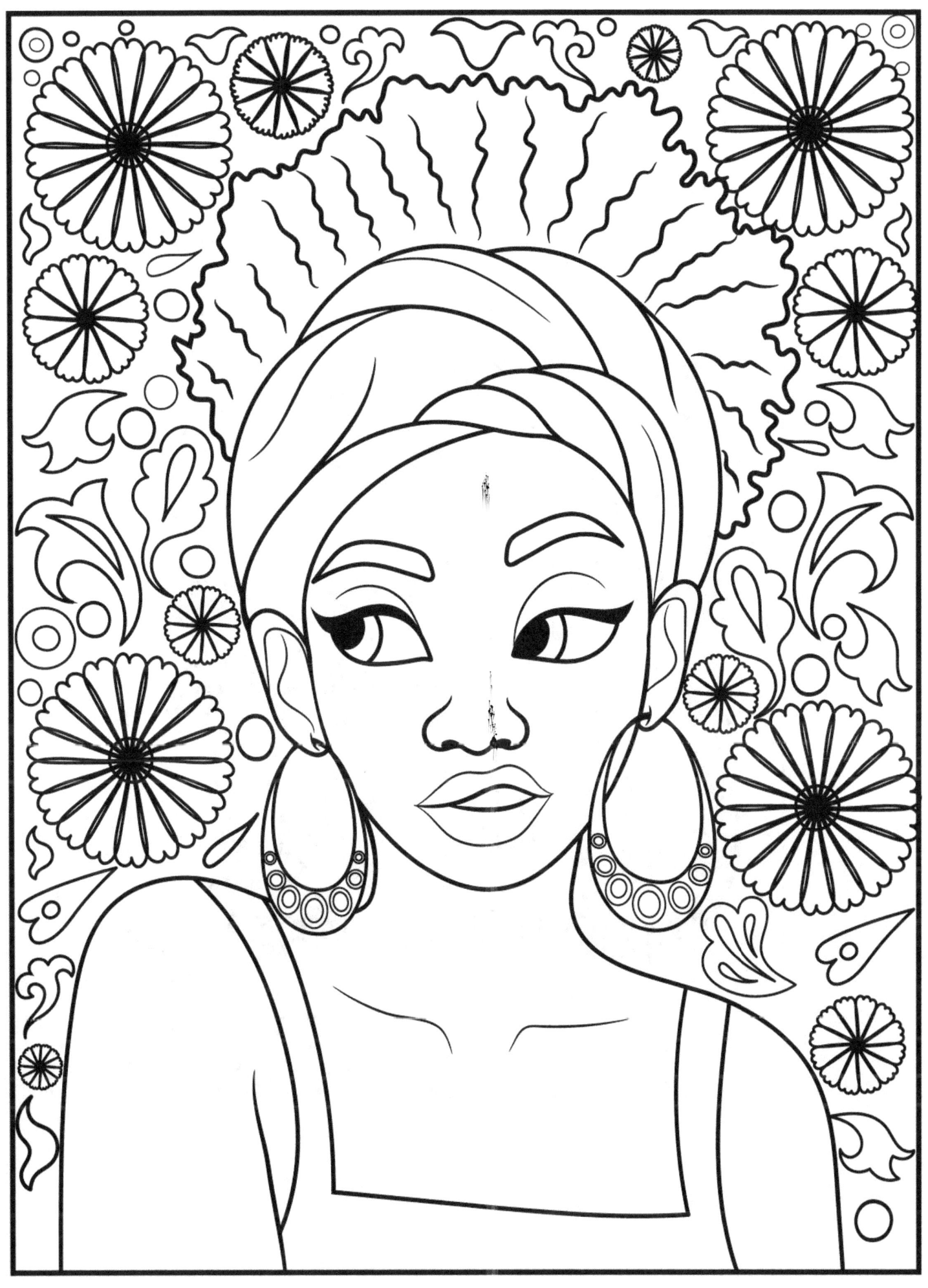

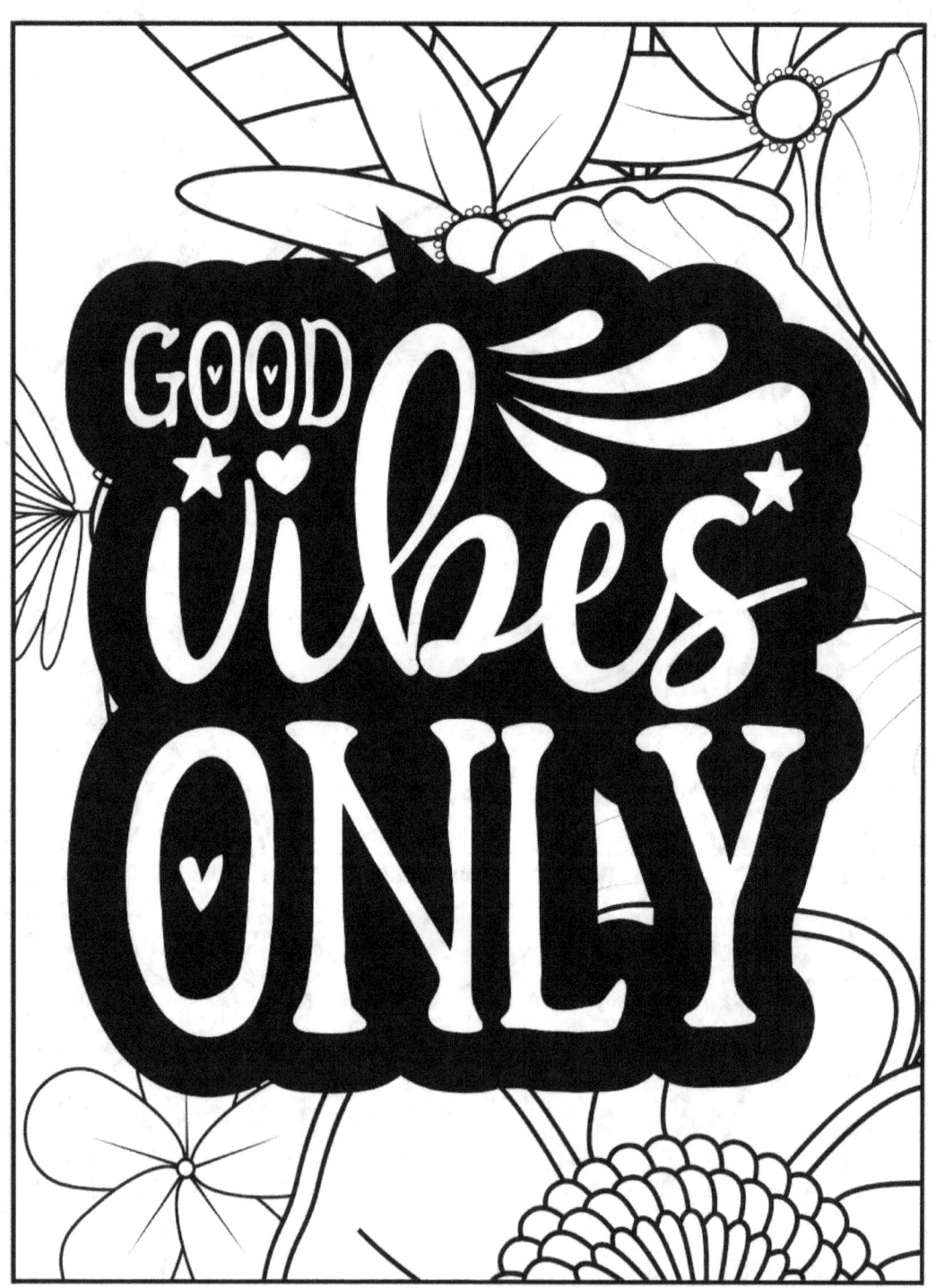

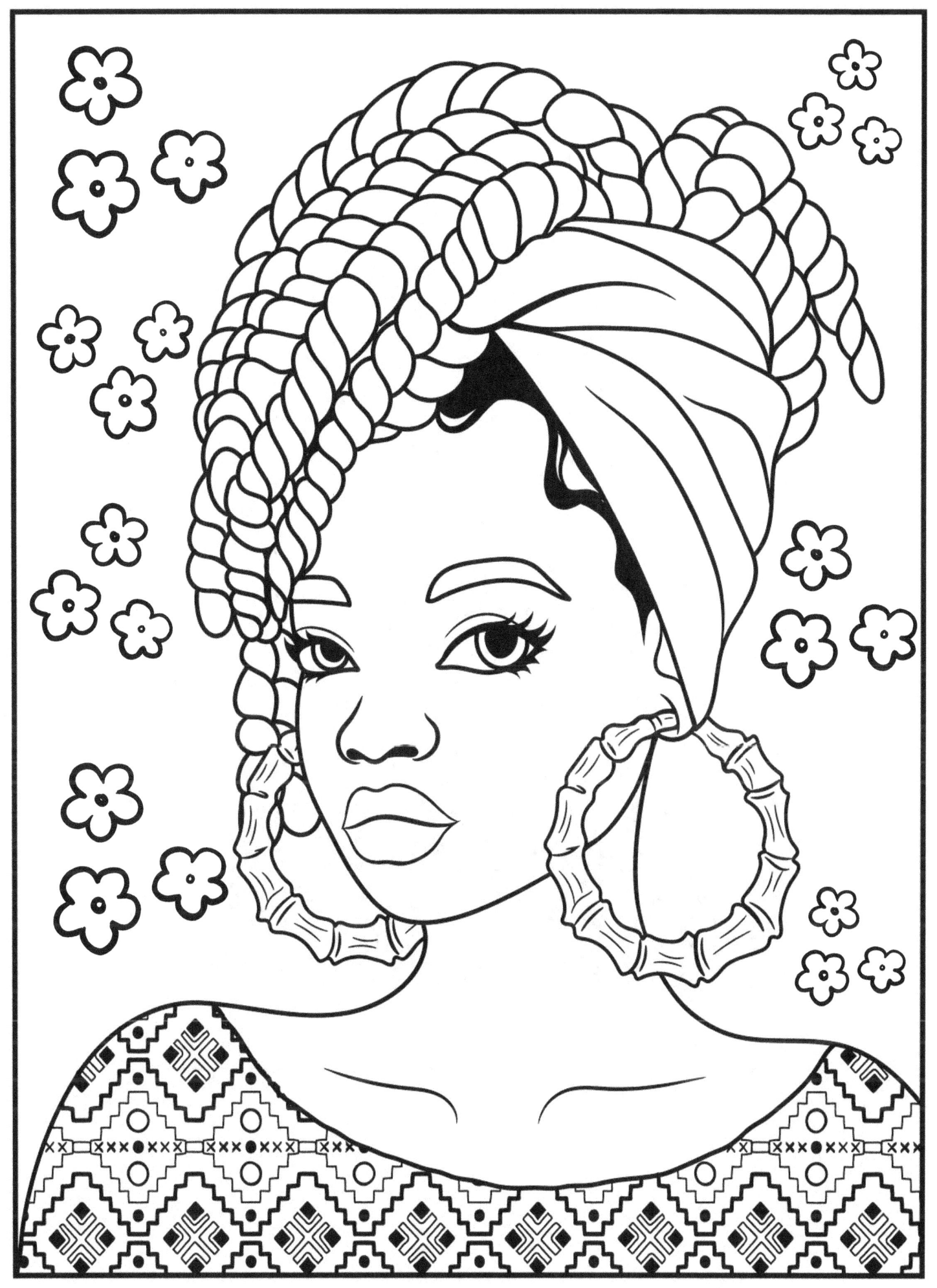

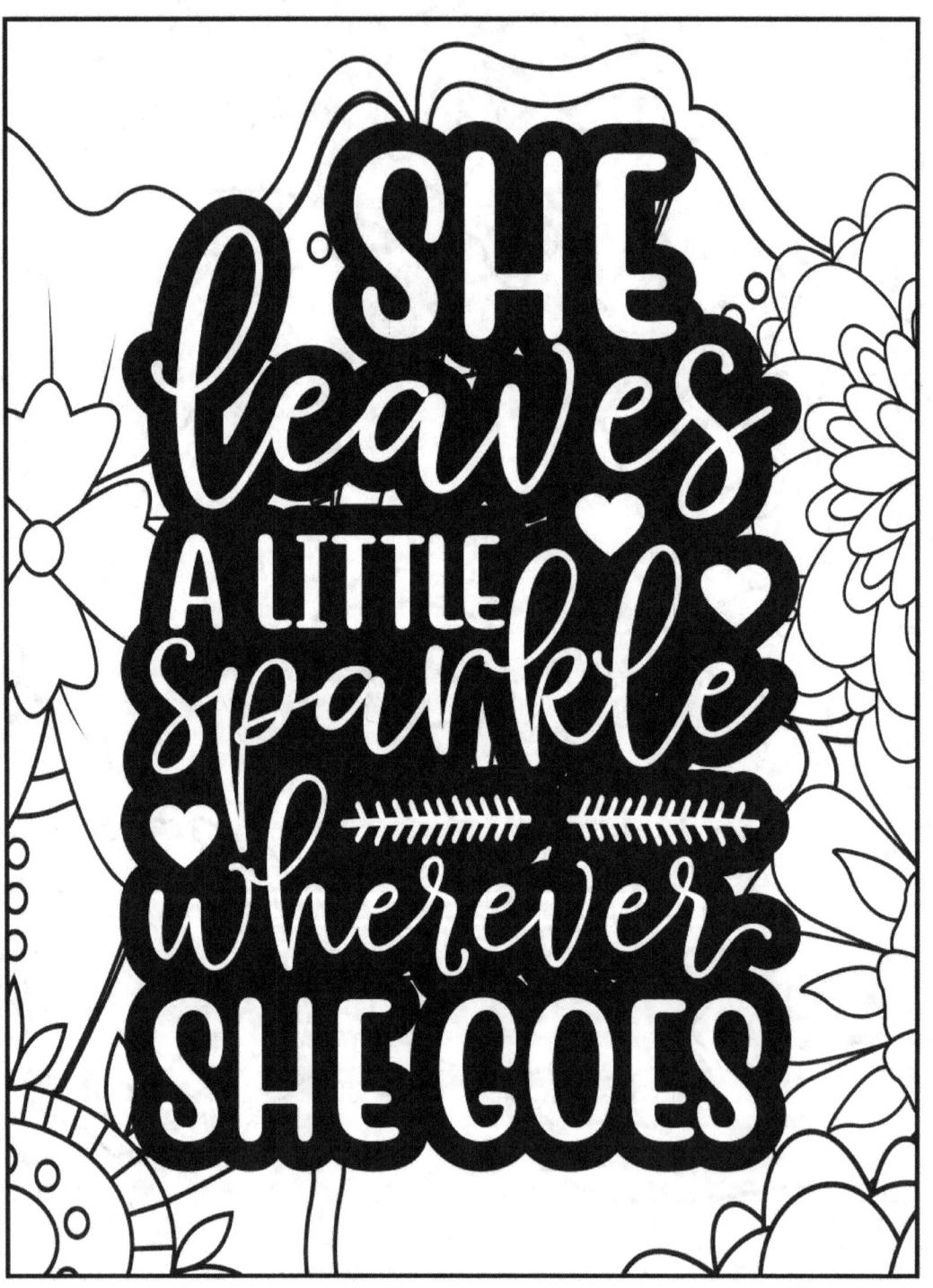

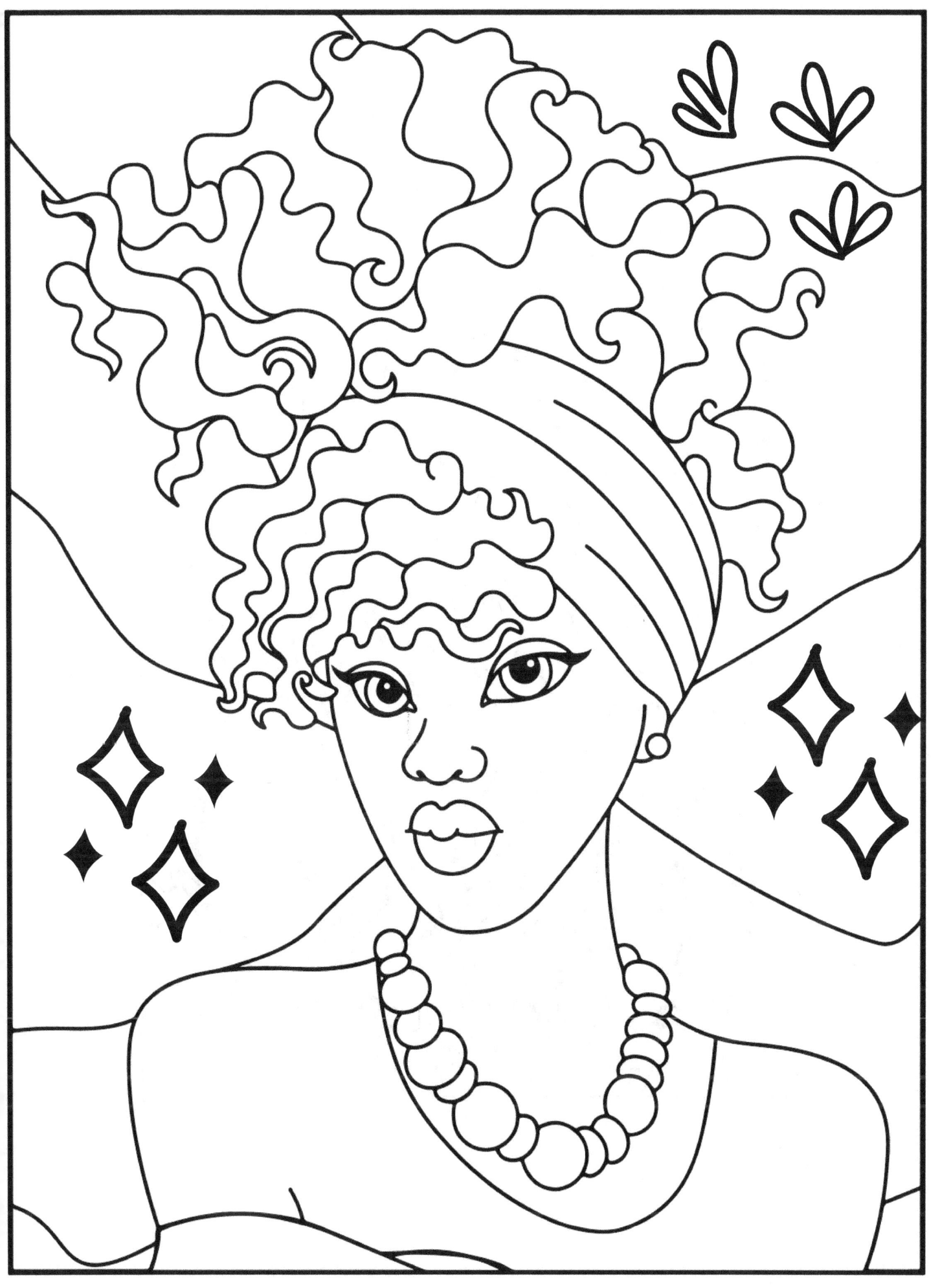

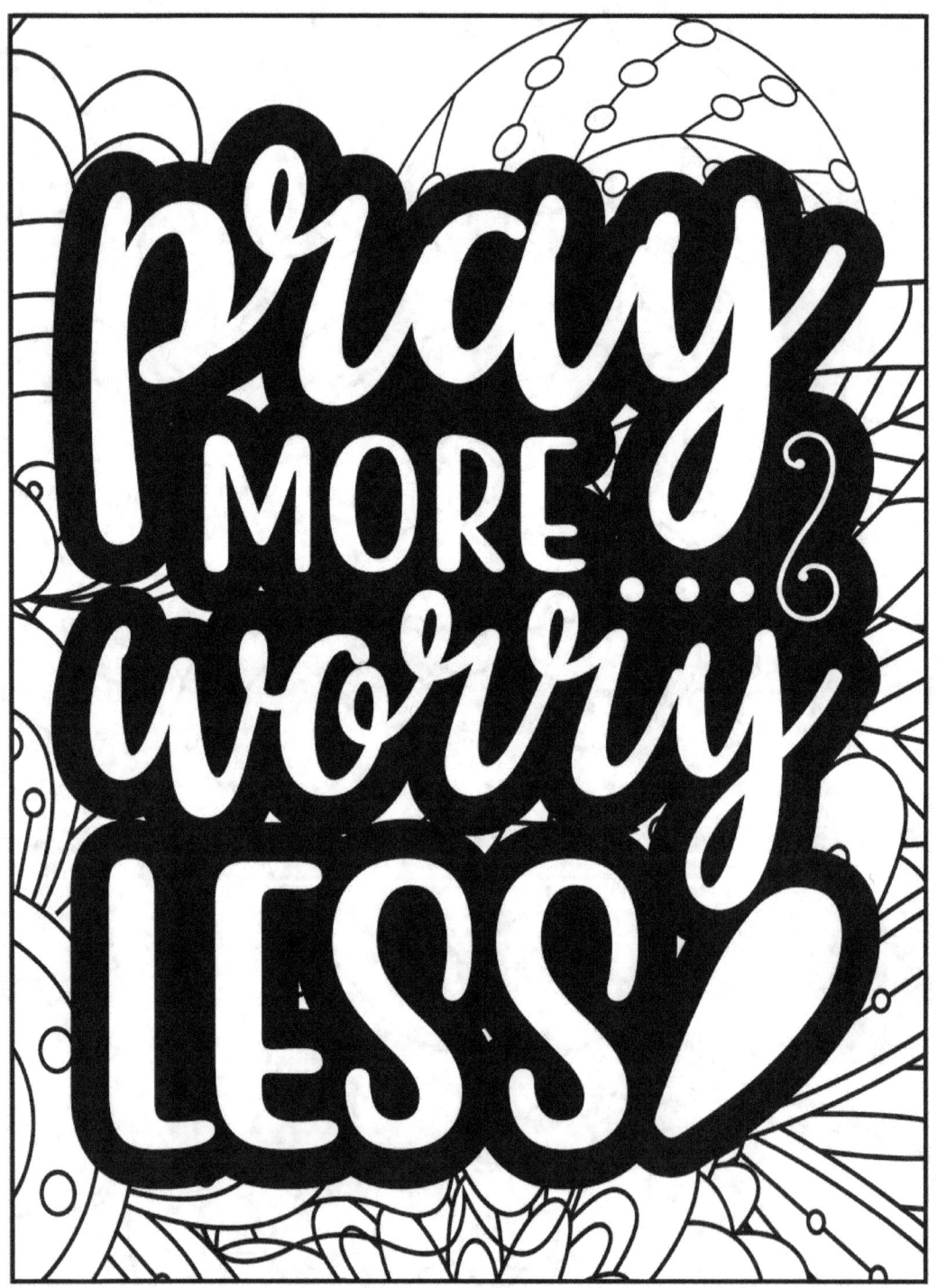

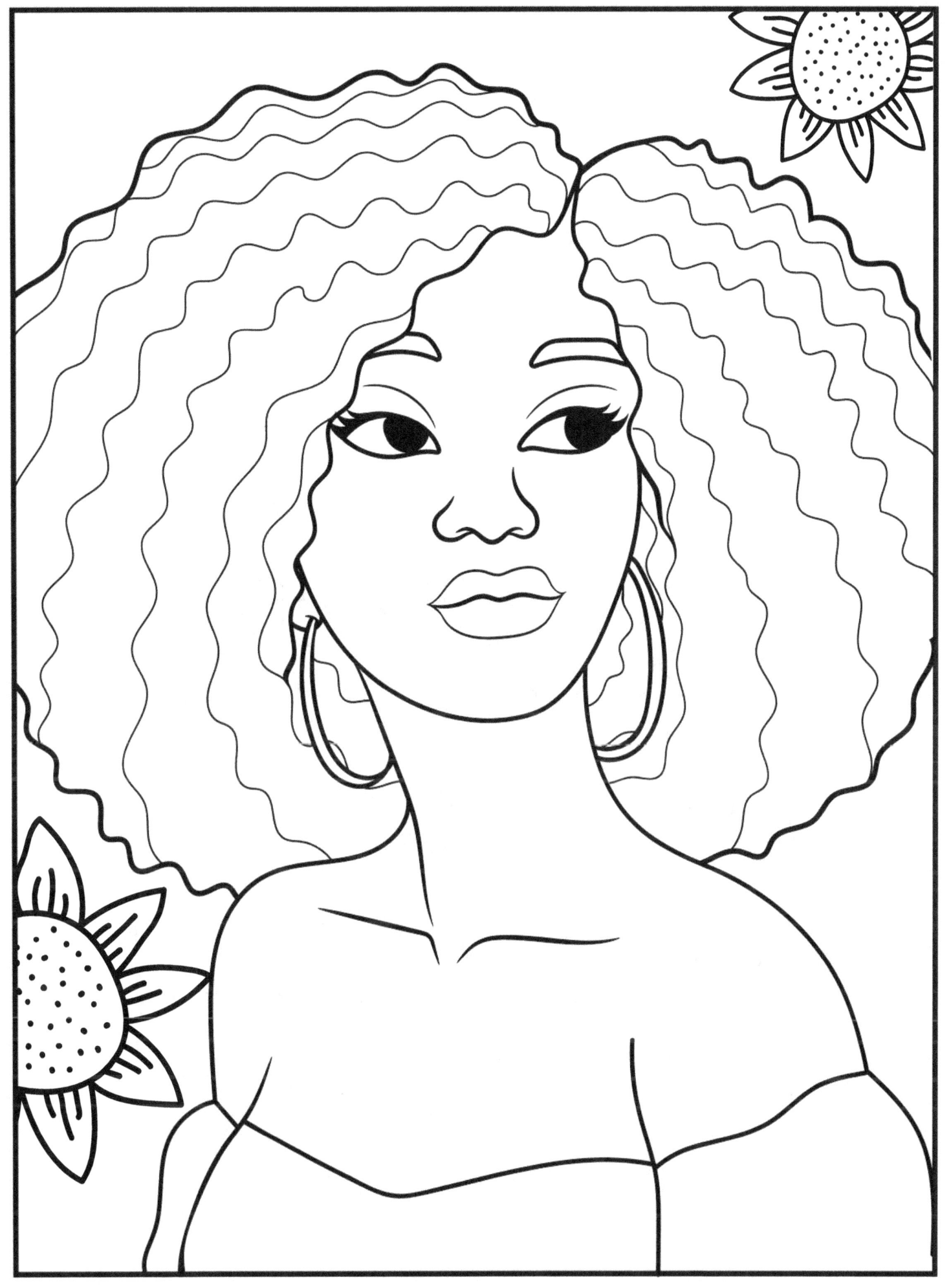

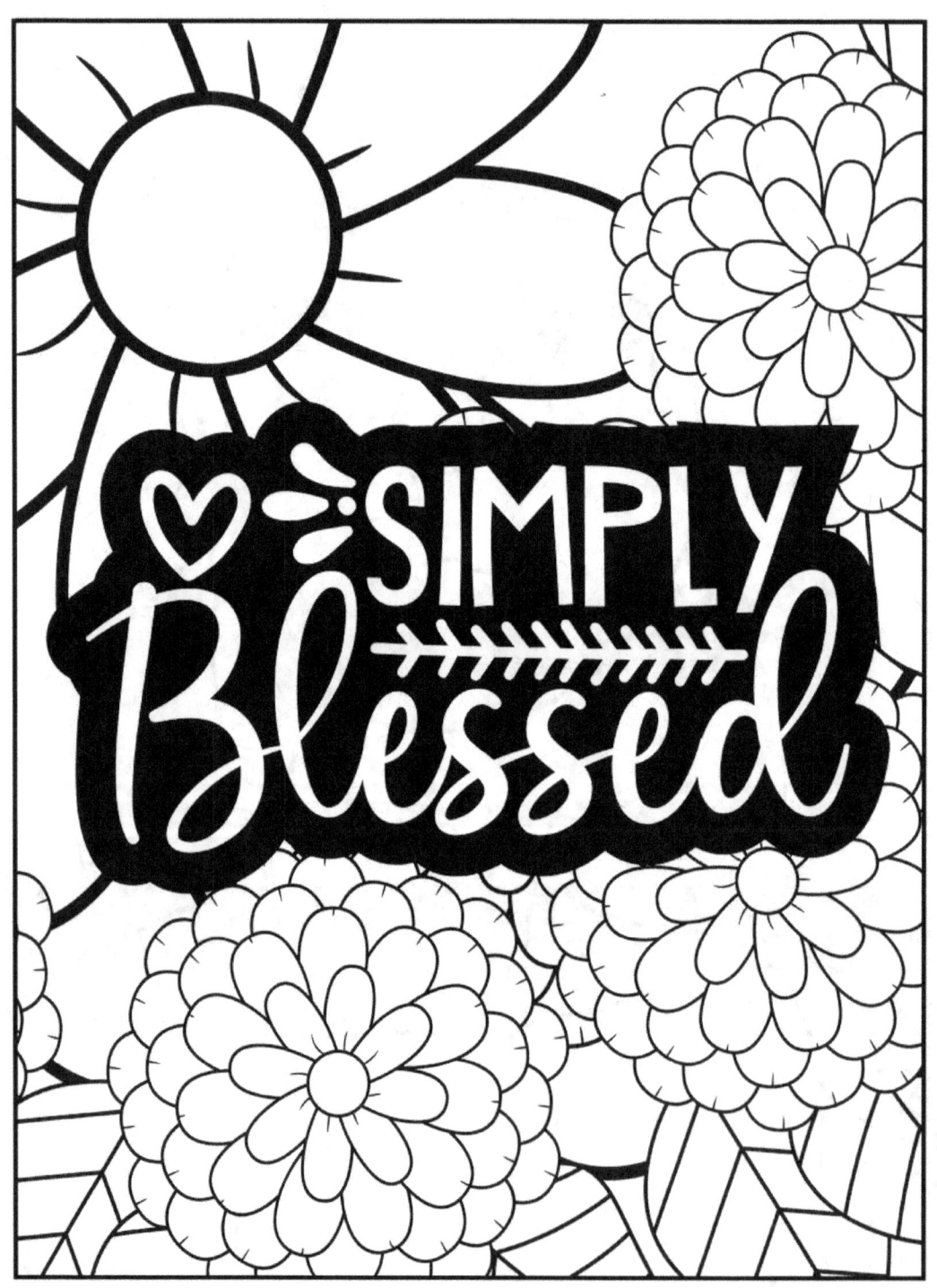

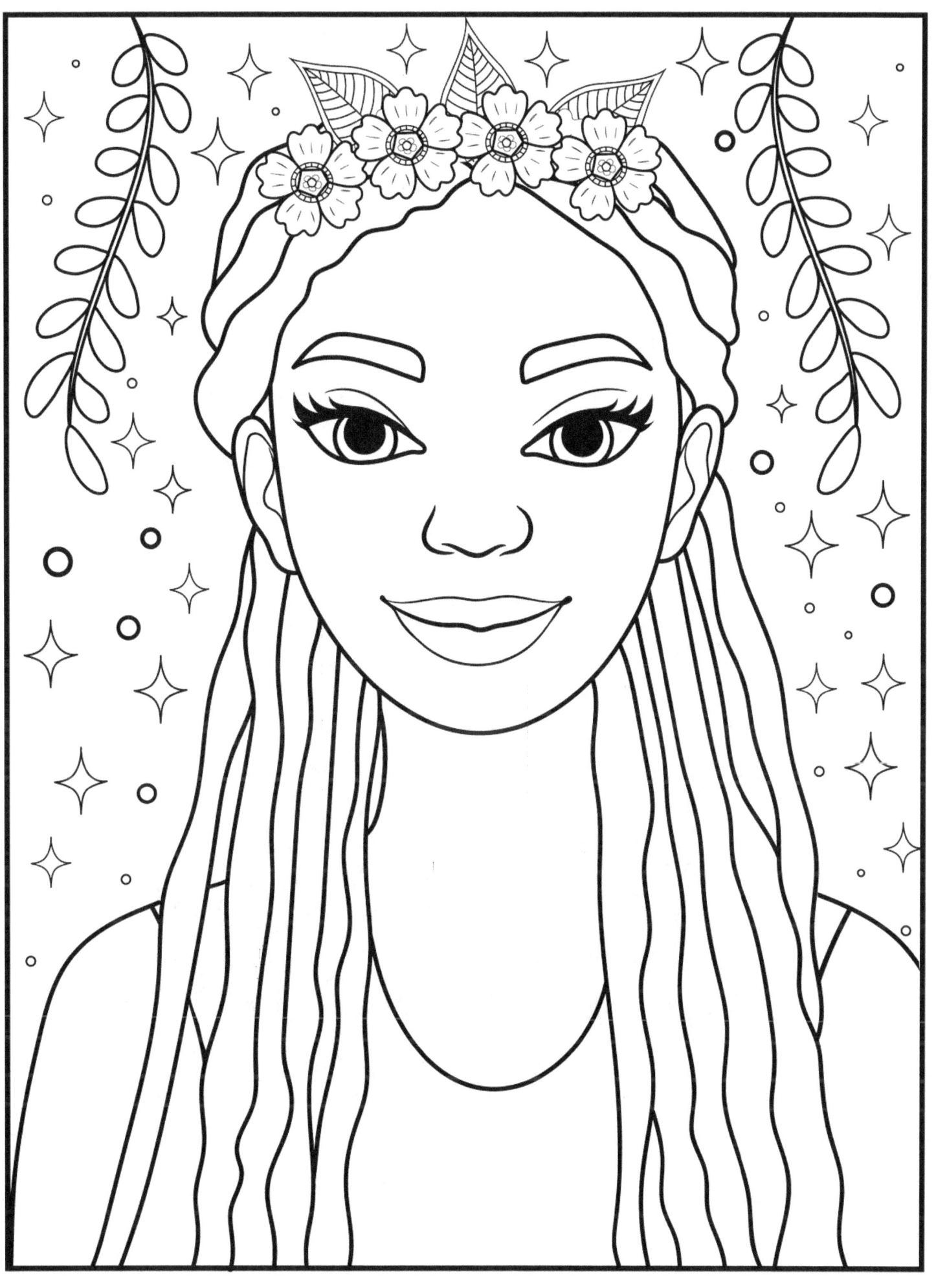

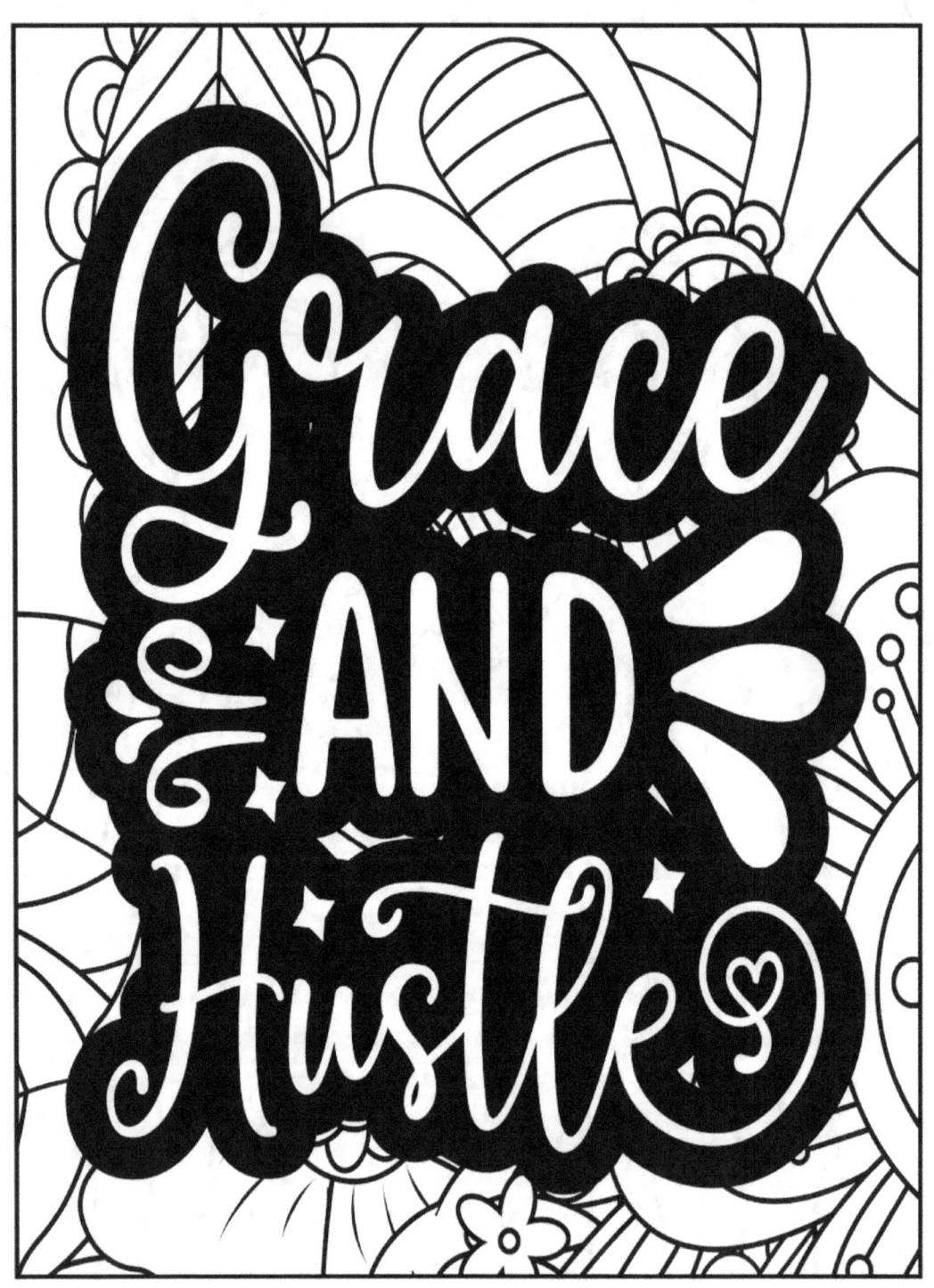

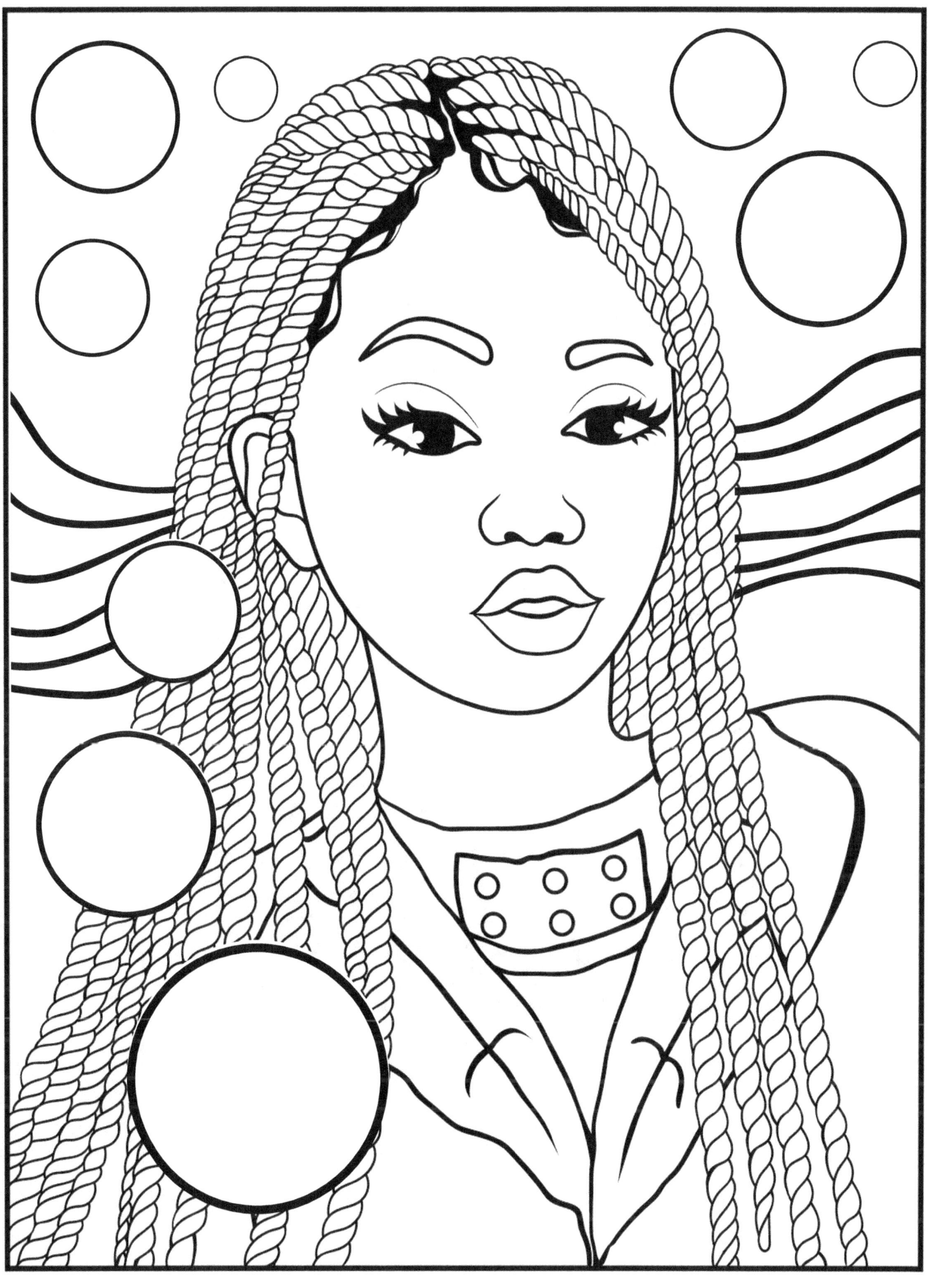

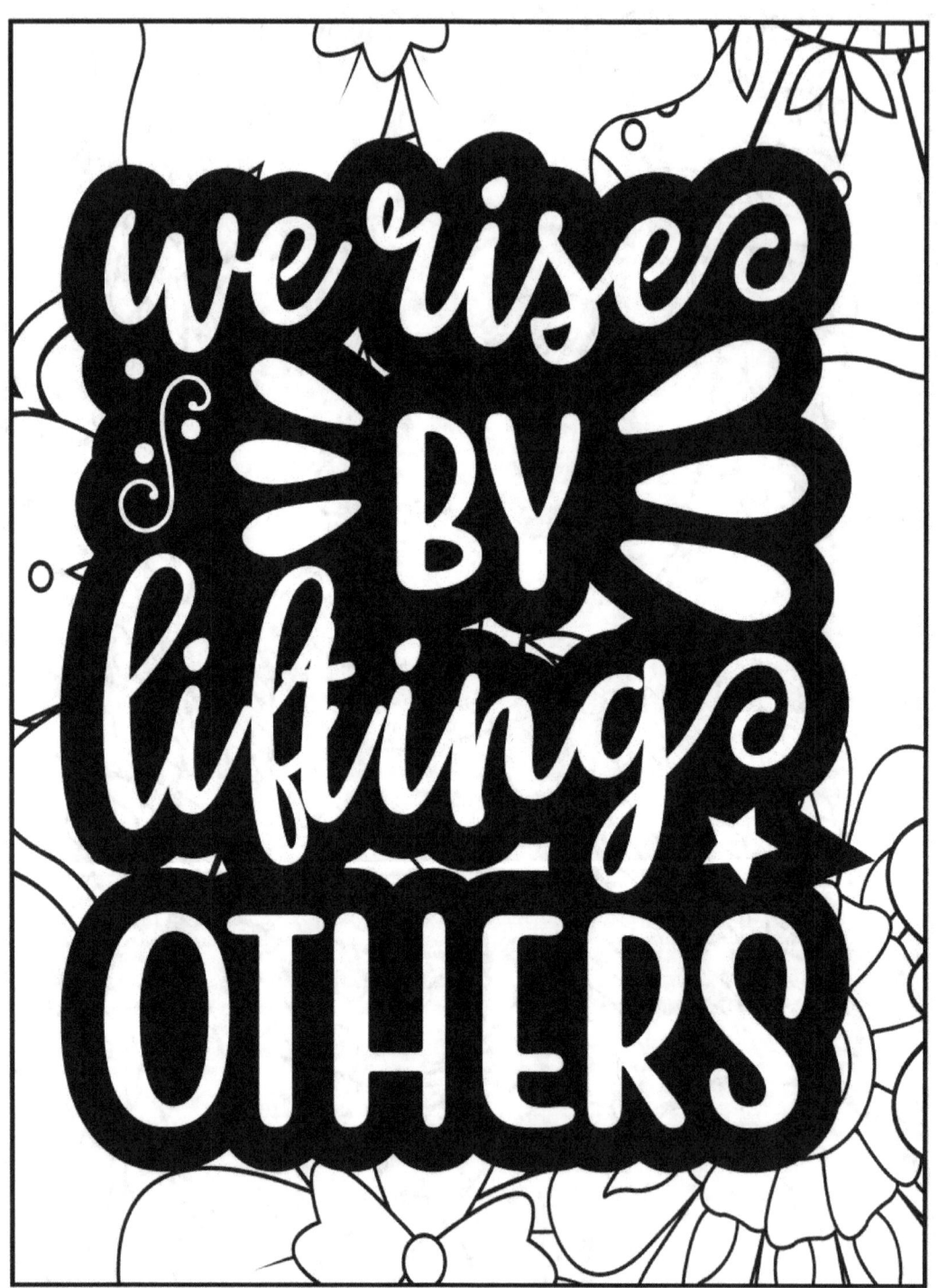

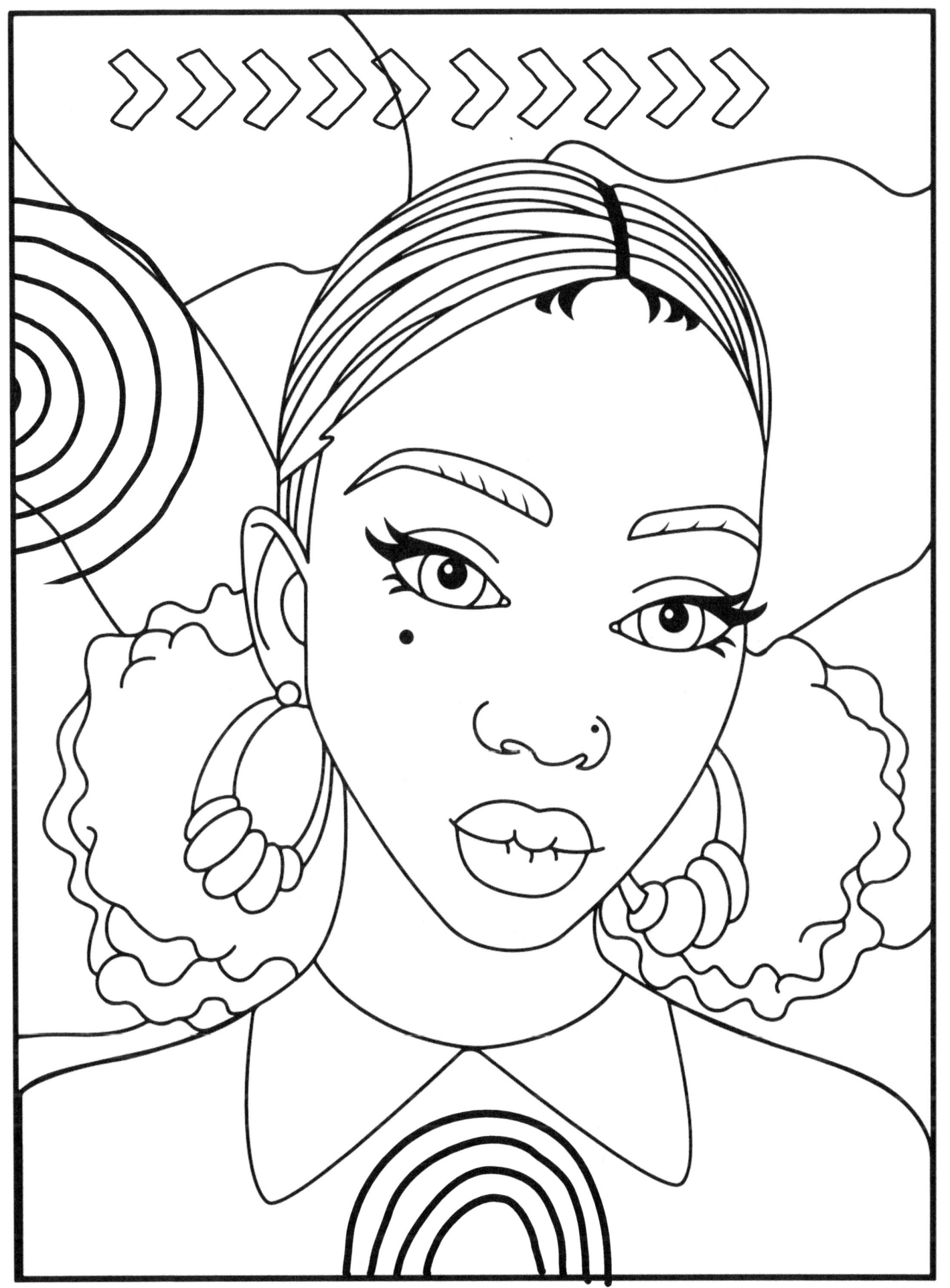

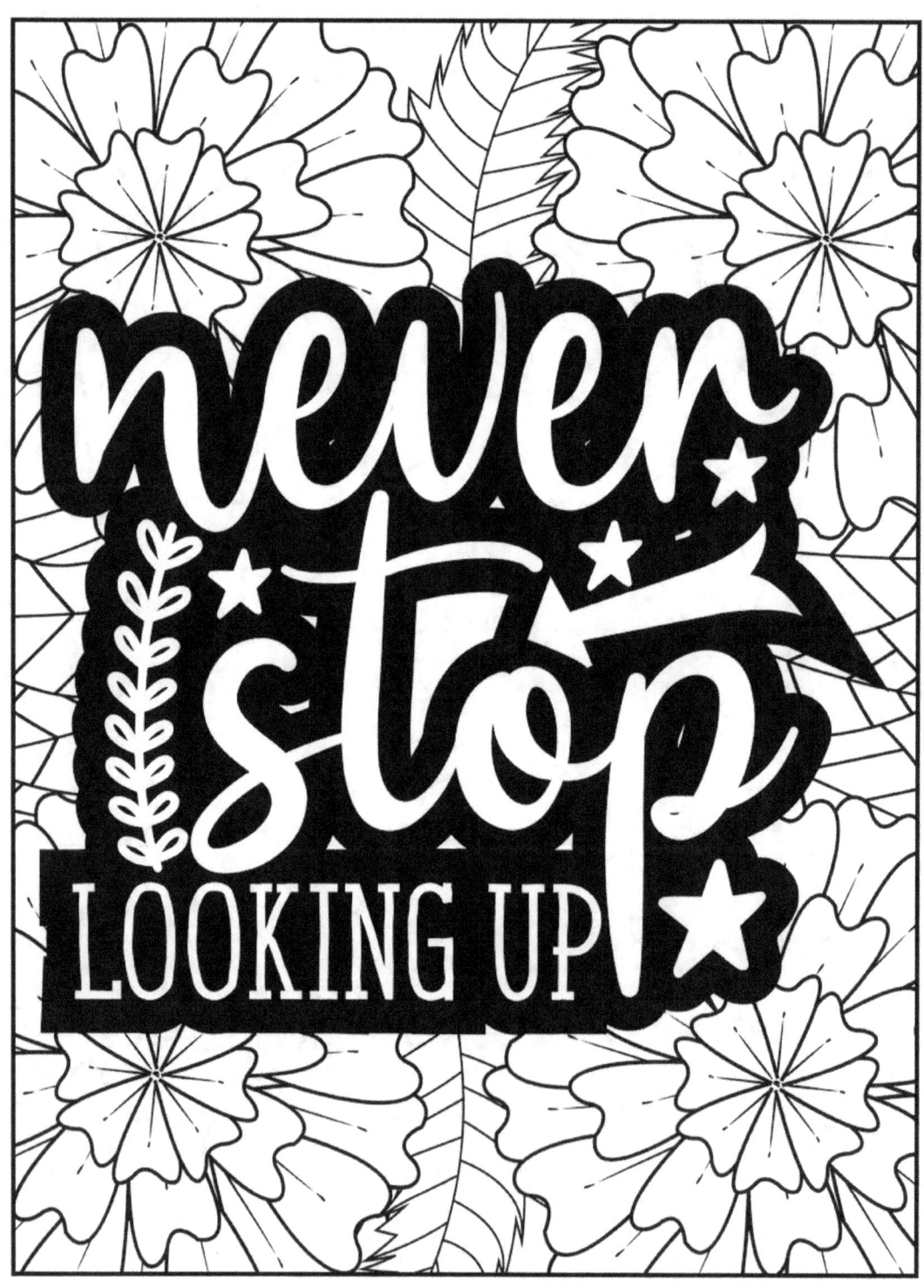

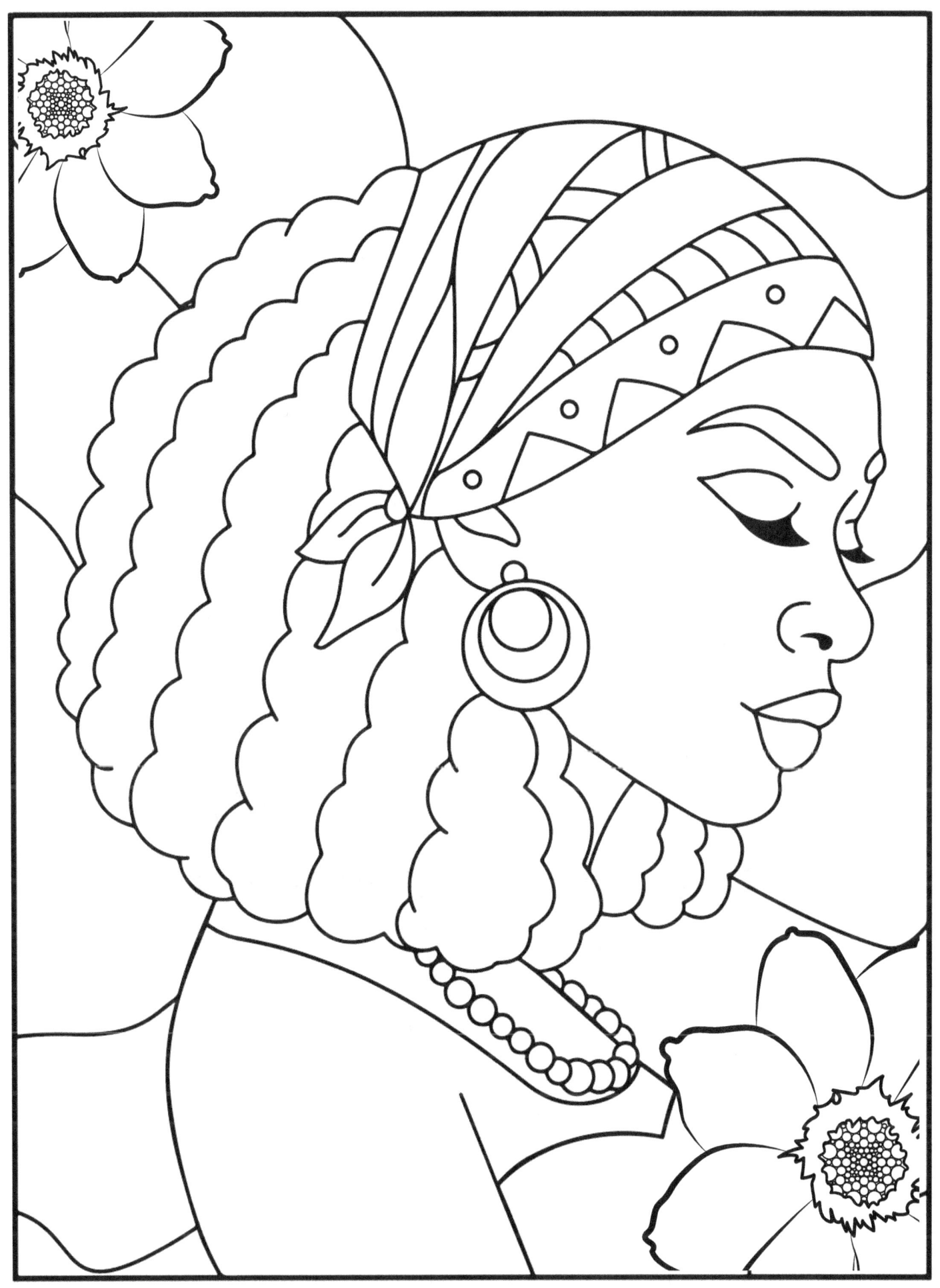

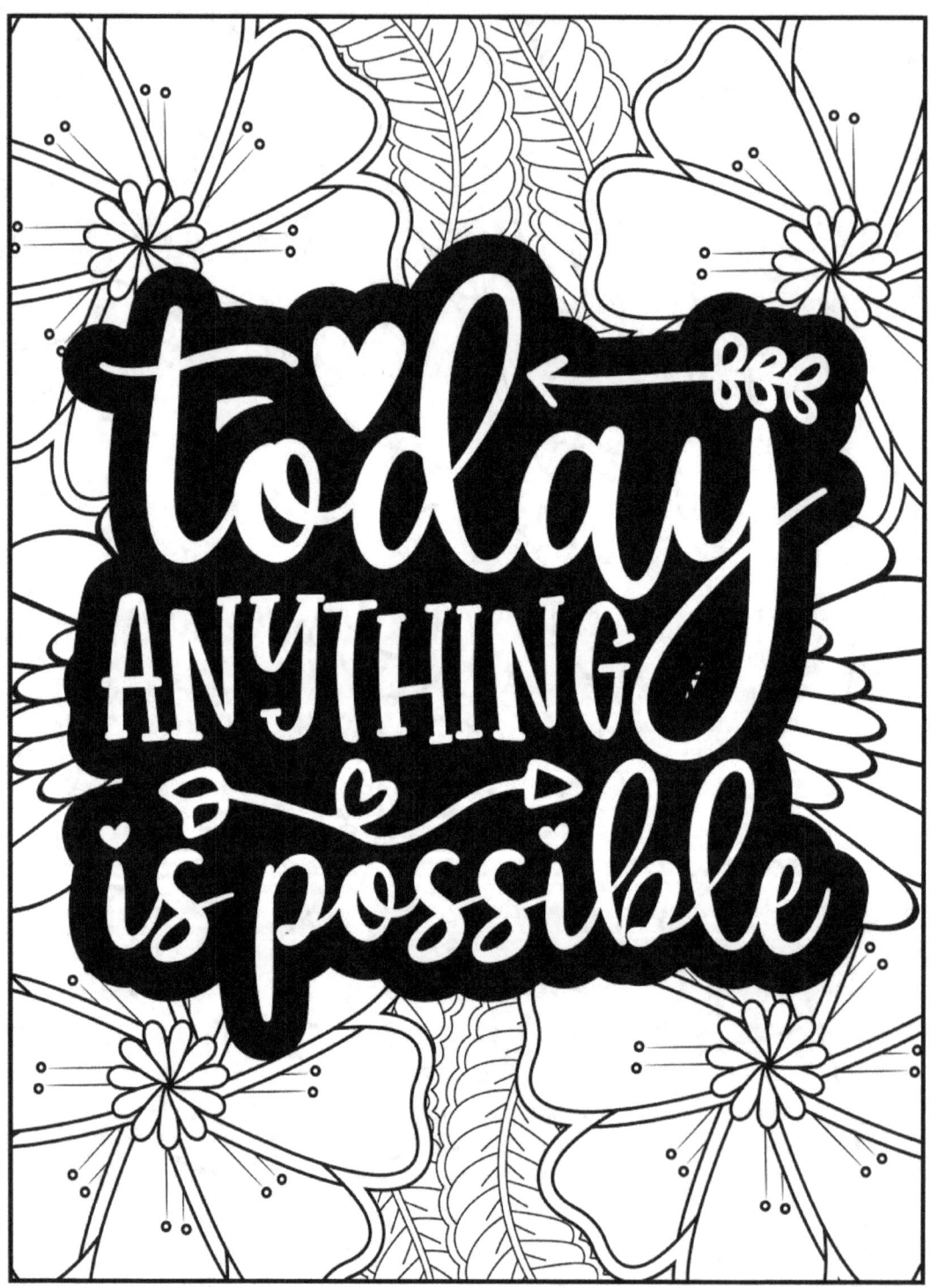

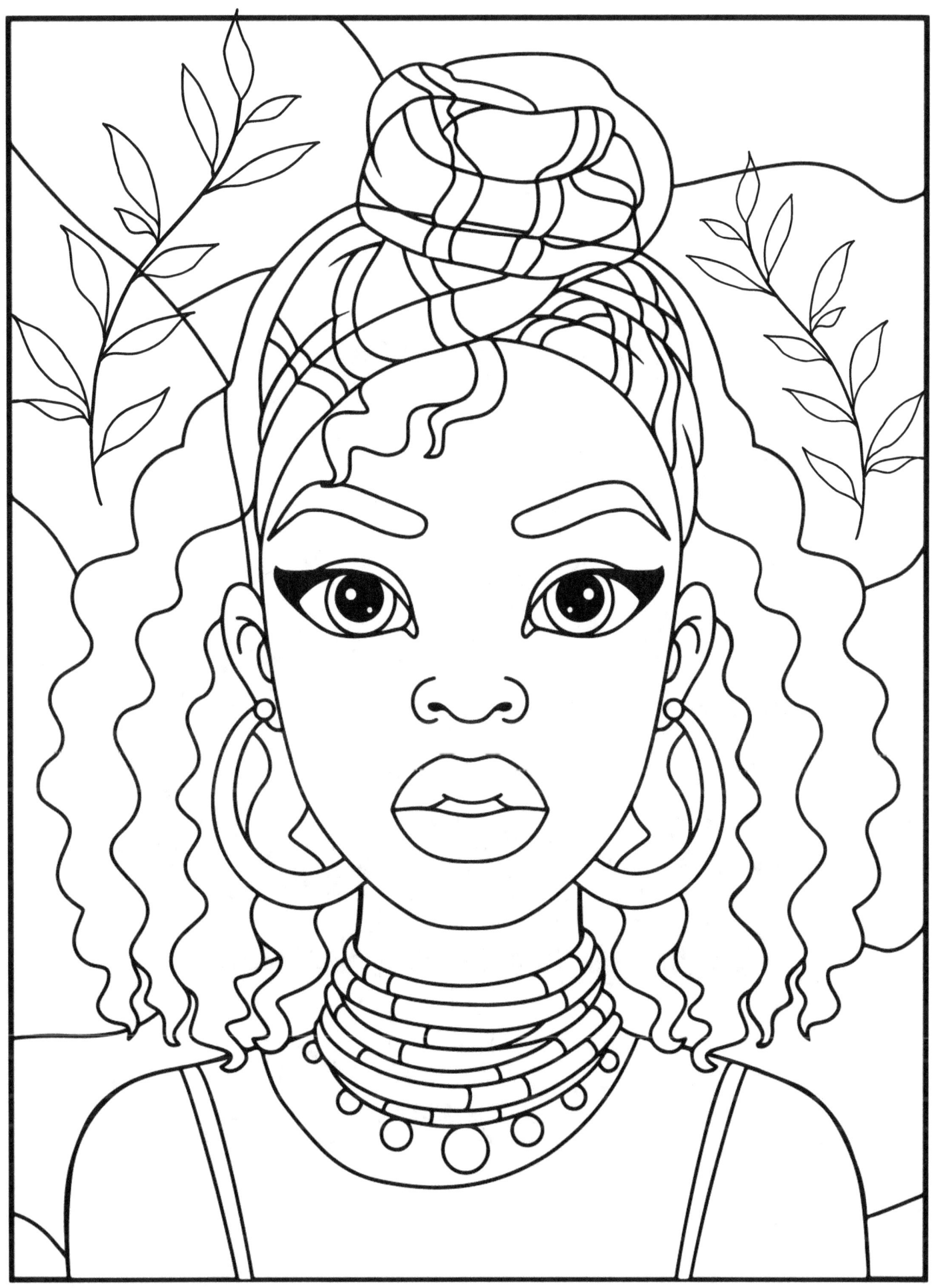

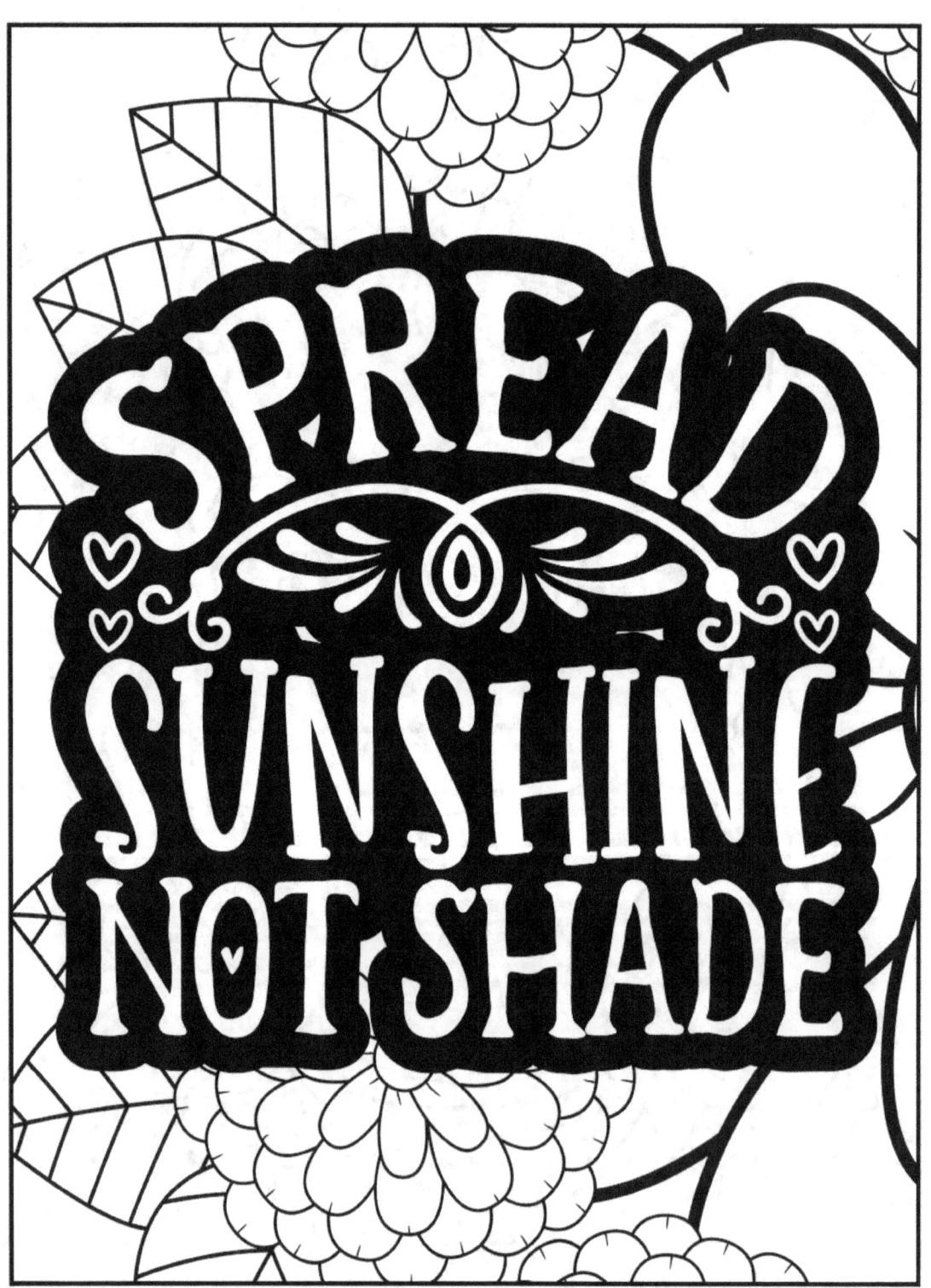

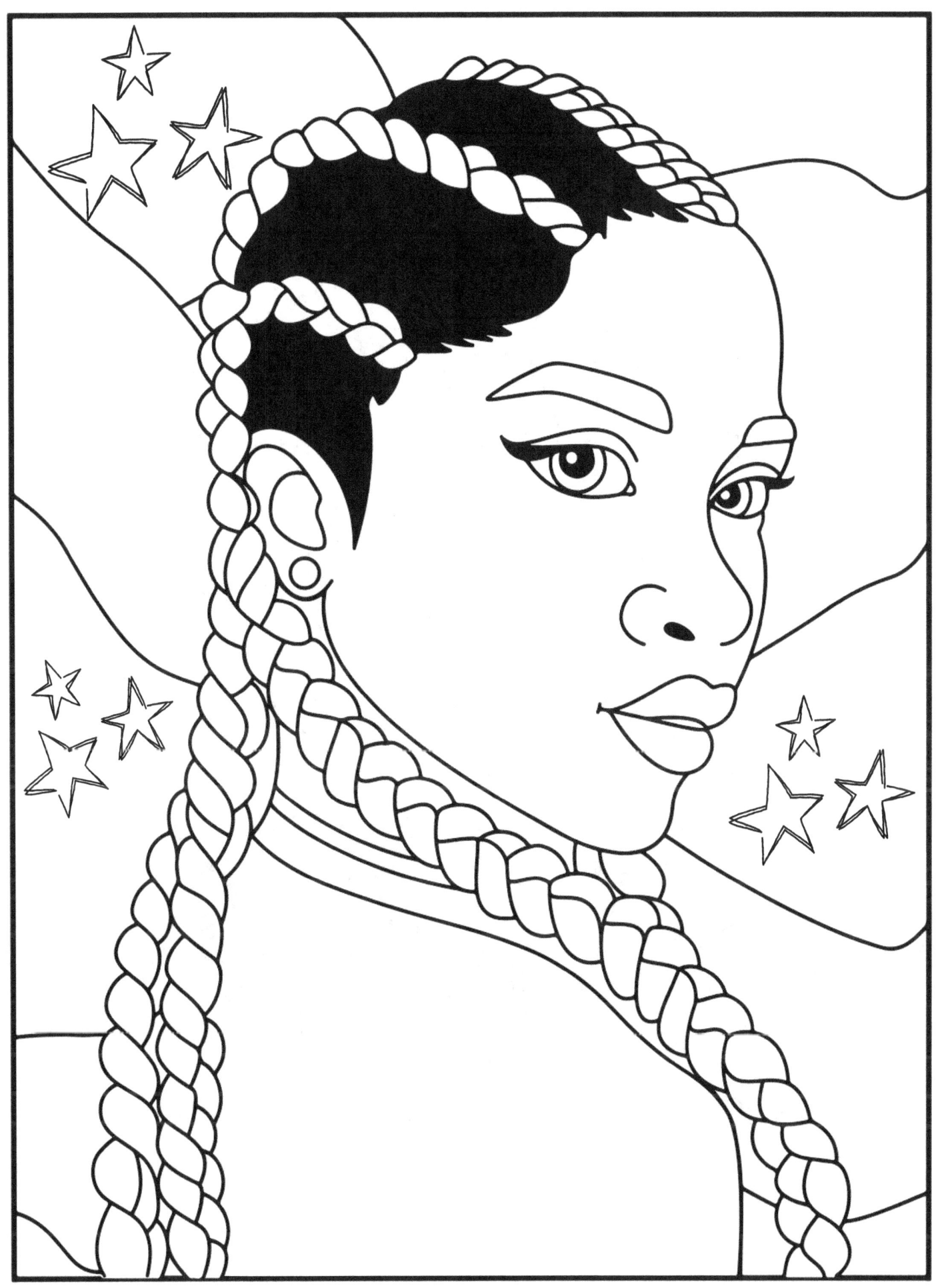

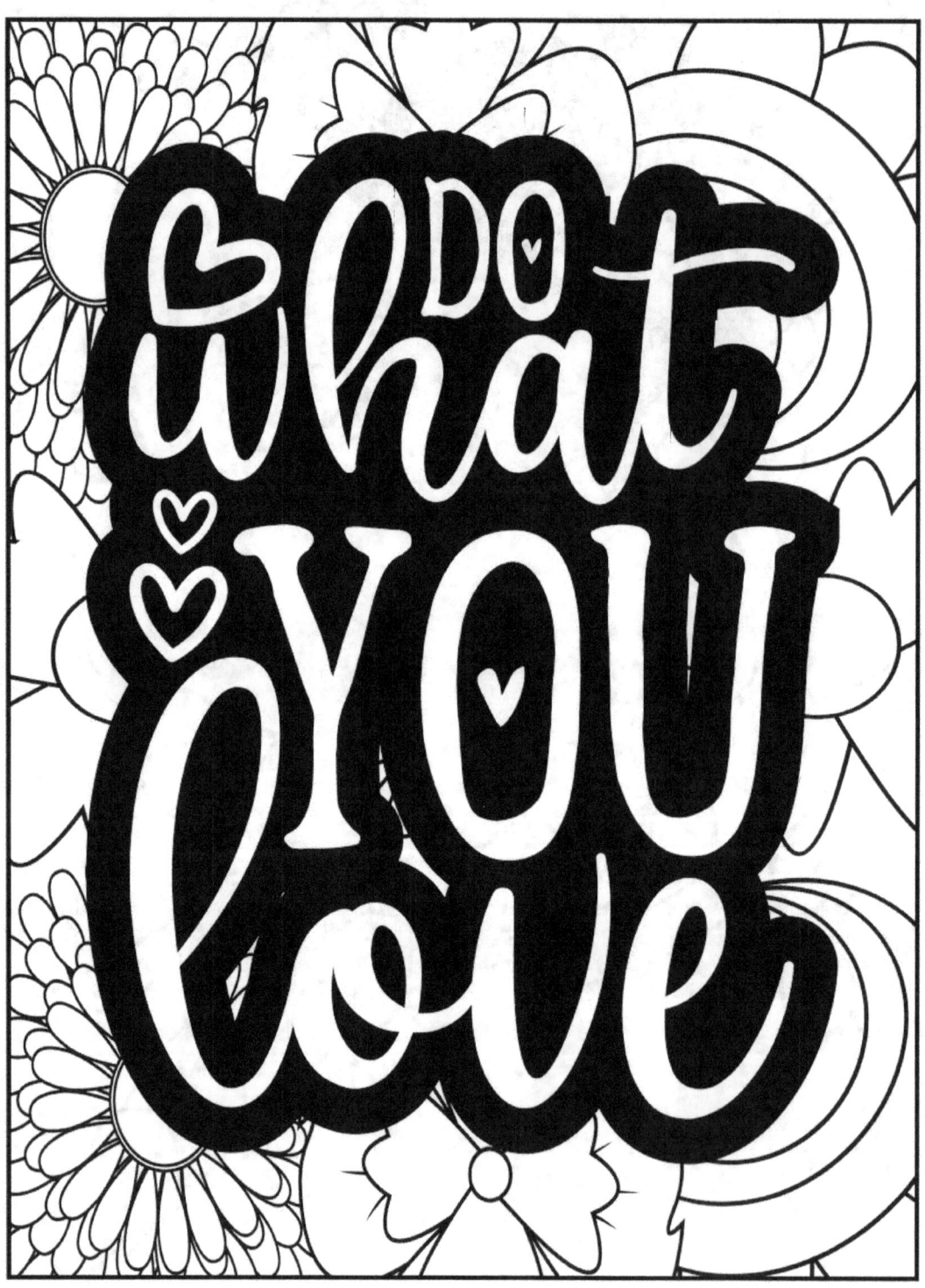

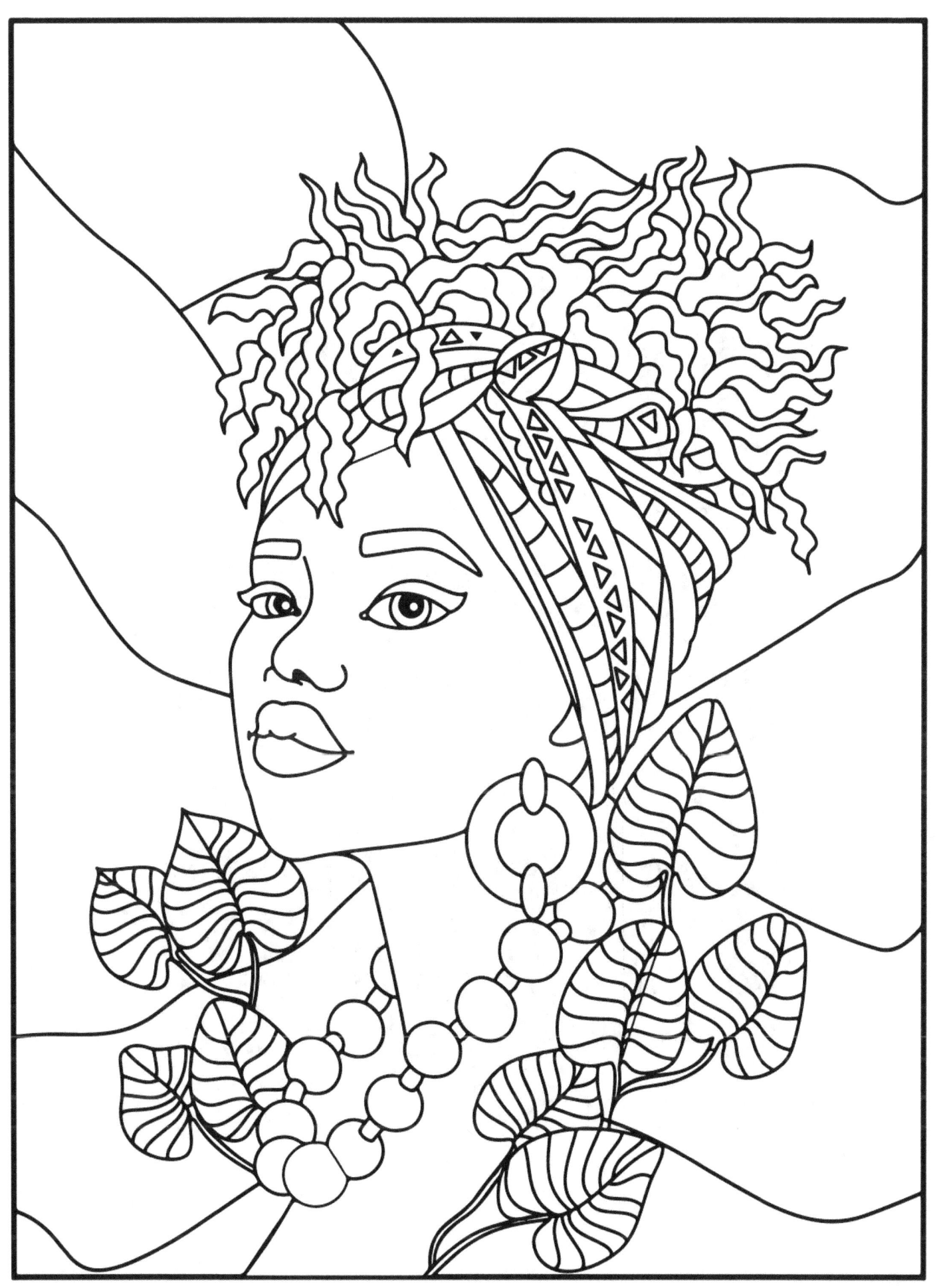

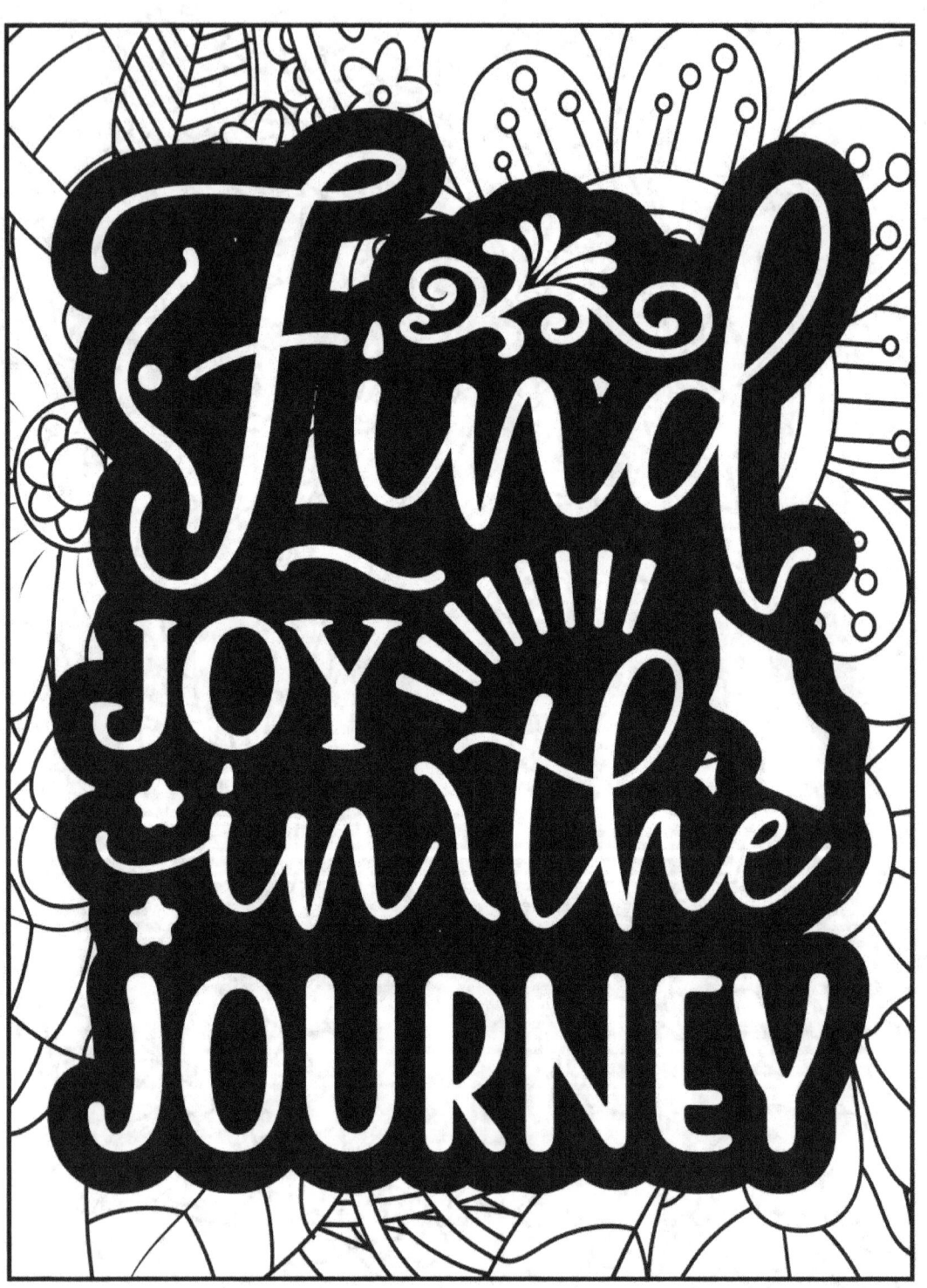

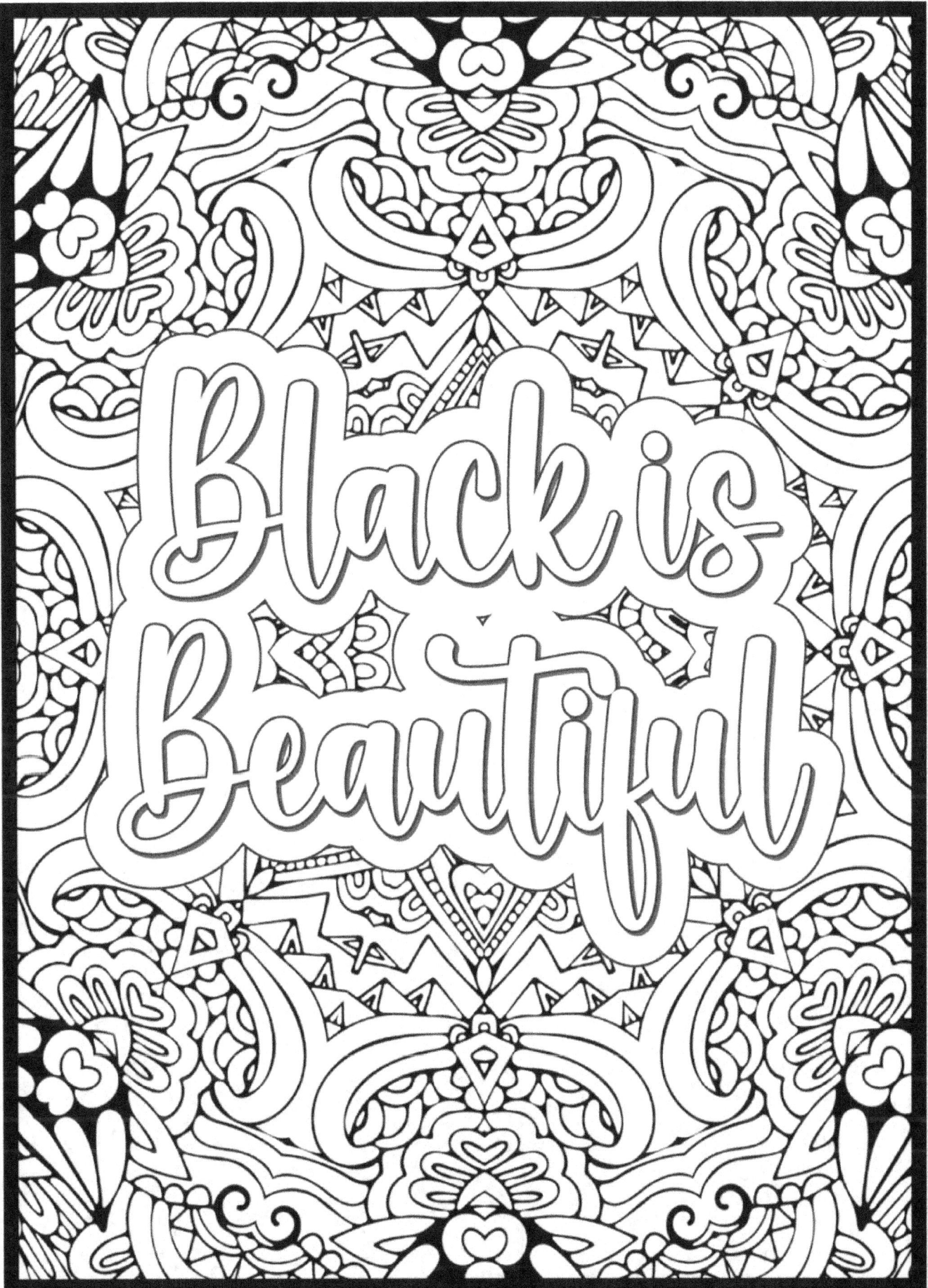

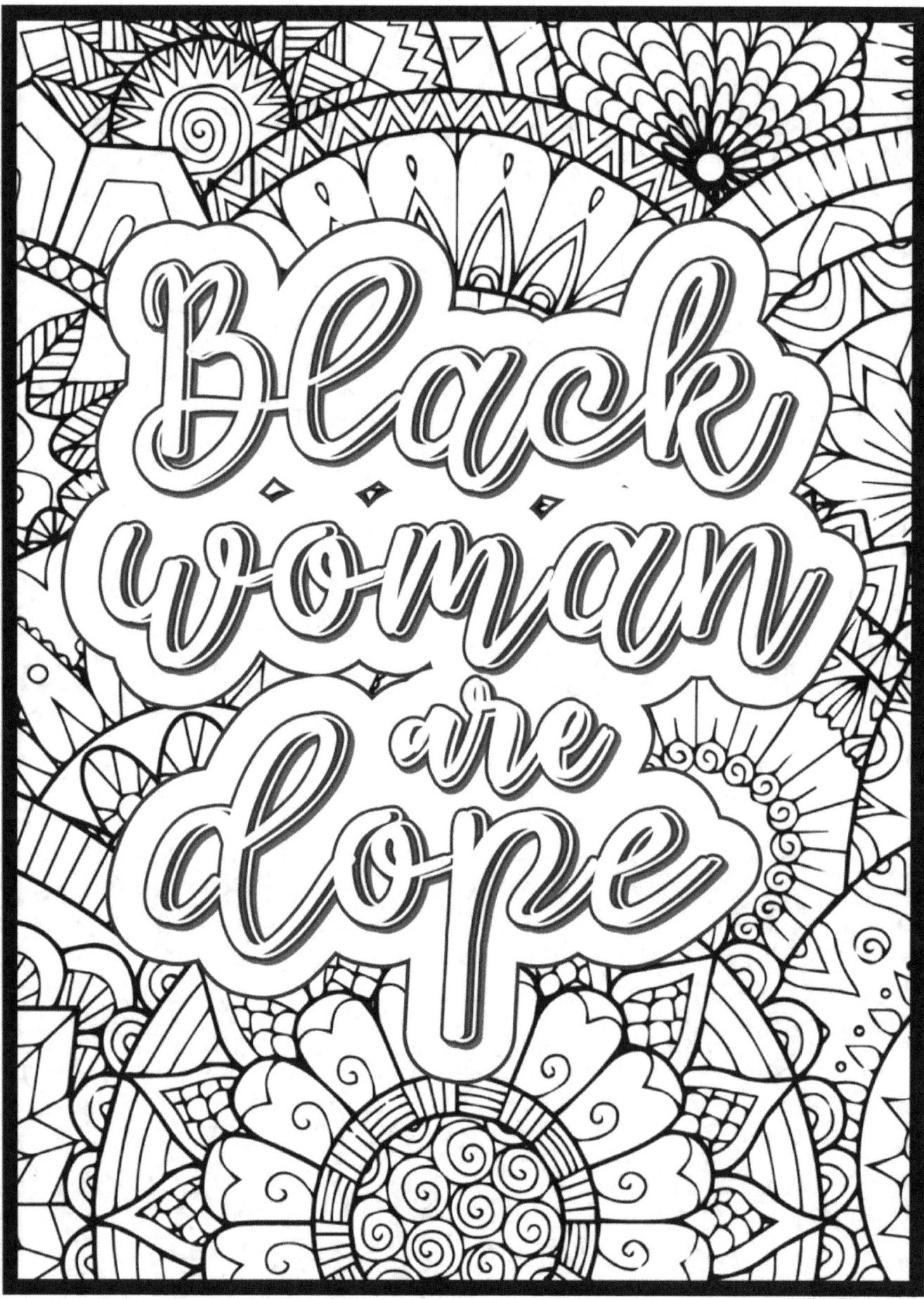

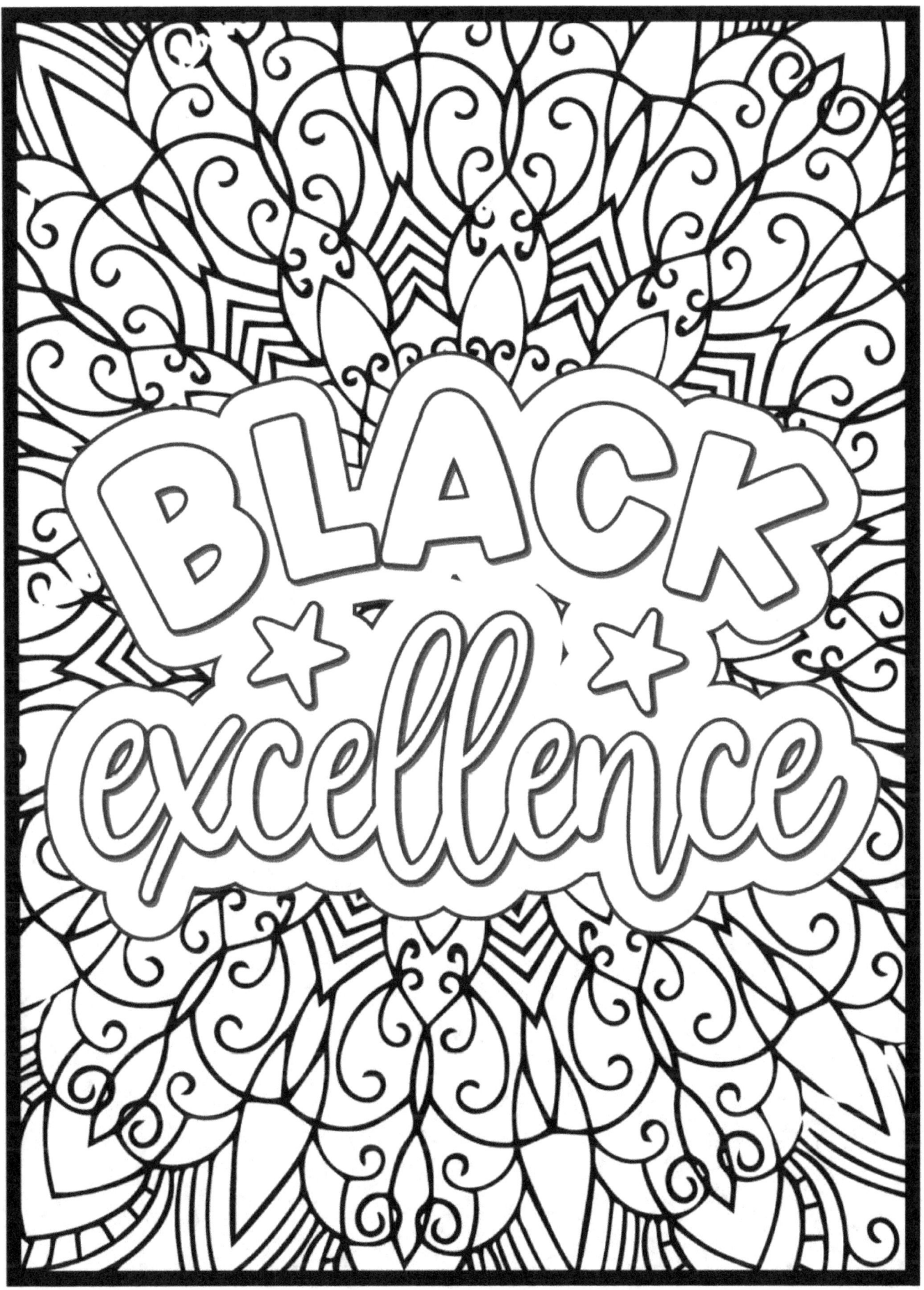

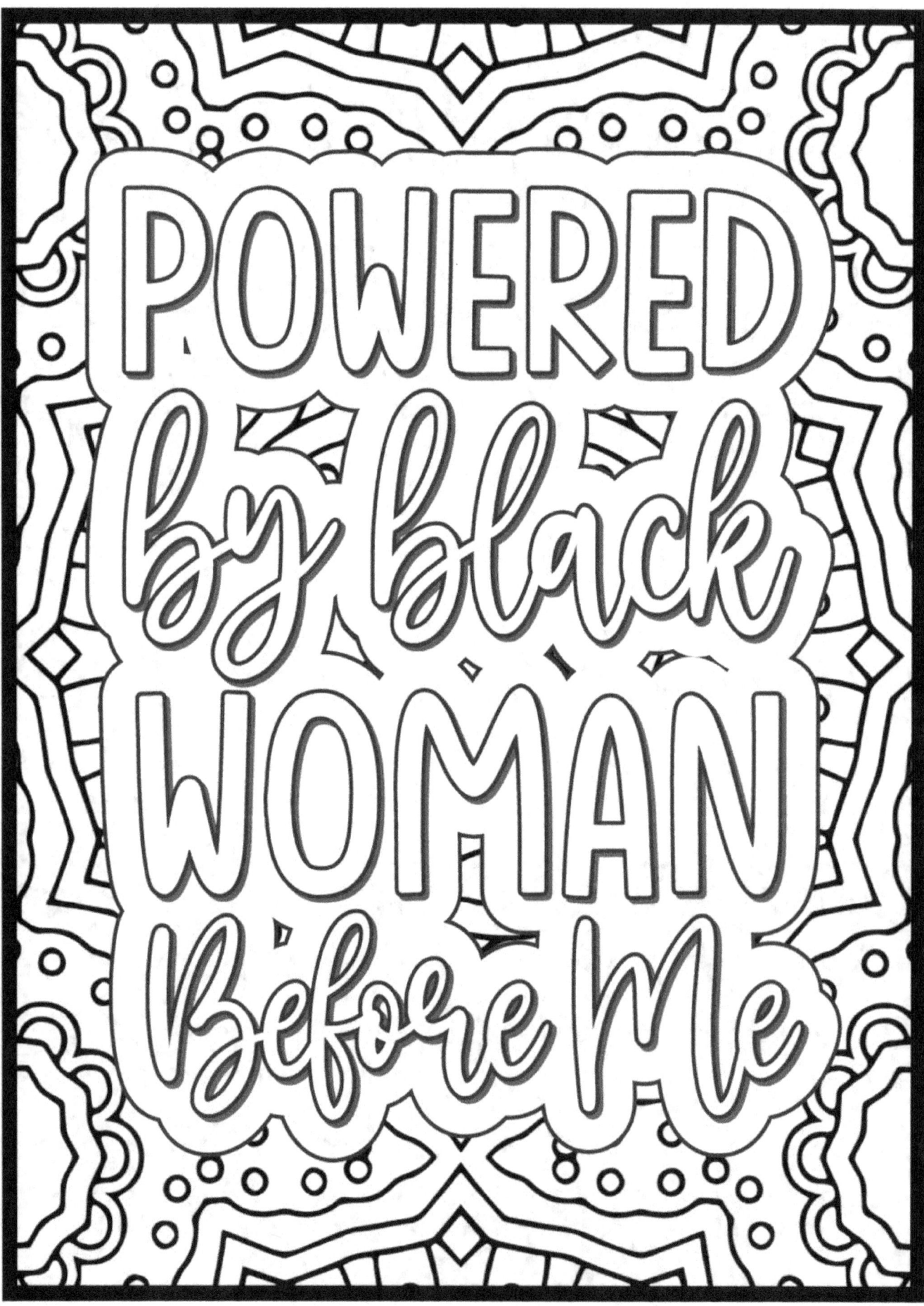

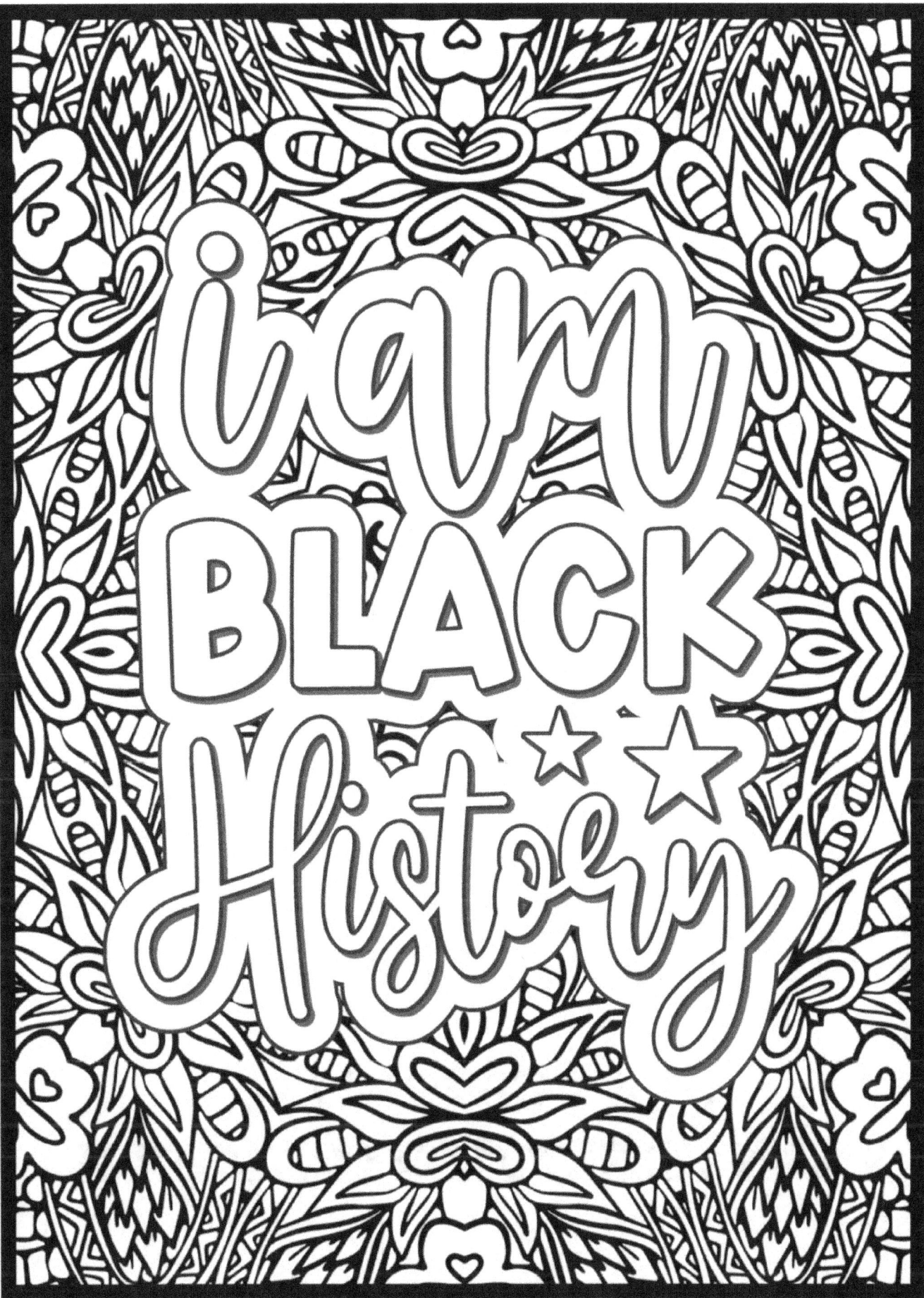

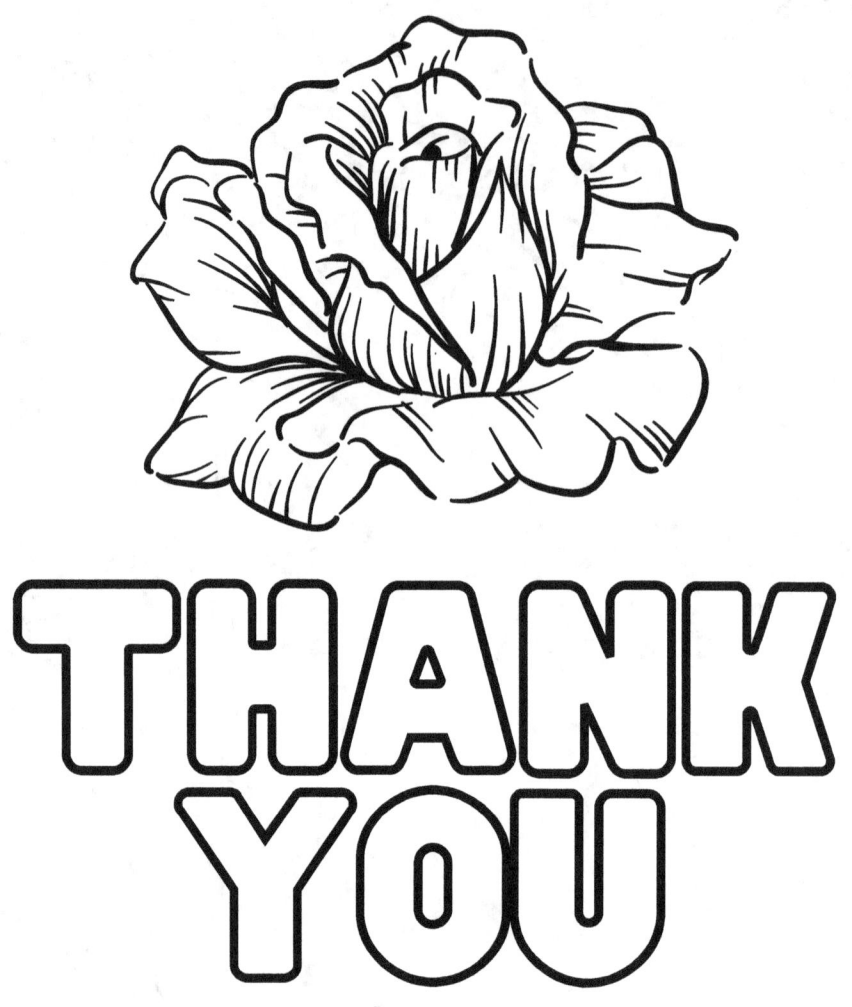

THANK YOU

FOR COLORING WITH ME!

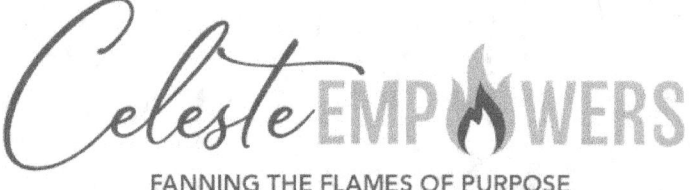

STAY CONNECTED
WWW.CELESTEEMPOWERS.COM